FILMMAKERS SERIES
edited by
ANTHONY SLIDE

1. *James Whale*, by James Curtis. 1982
2. *Cinema Stylists*, by John Belton. 1983
3. *Harry Langdon*, by William Schelly. 1982
4. *William A. Wellman*, by Frank Thompson. 1983
5. *Stanley Donen*, by Joseph Casper. 1983
6. *Brian DePalma*, by Michael Bliss. 1983
7. *J. Stuart Blackton*, by Marian Blackton Trimble. 1985
8. *Martin Scorsese and Michael Cimino*, by Michael Bliss. 1985
9. *Franklin J. Schaffner*, by Erwin Kim. 1985
10. *D. W. Griffith at Biograph*, by Cooper C. Graham et al. 1985
11. *Some Day We'll Laugh: An Autobiography*, by Esther Ralston. 1985
12. *The Memoirs of Alice Guy Blach*, trans. by Roberta and Simone Blaché. 1986
13. *Leni Riefenstahl and Olympia*, by Cooper C. Graham. 1986
14. *Robert Florey*, by Brian Taves. 1987
15. *Henry King's America*, by Walter Coppedge. 1986
16. *Aldous Huxley and Film*, by Virginia M. Clark. 1987
17. *Five American Cinematographers*, by Scott Eyman. 1987
18. *Cinematographers on the Art and Craft of Cinematography*, by Anna Kate Sterling. 1987
19. *Stars of the Silents*, by Edward Wagenknecht. 1987
20. *Twentieth Century-Fox*, by Aubrey Solomon. 1988
21. *Highlights and Shadows: The Memoirs of a Hollywood Cameraman*, by Charles G. Clarke. 1989
22. *I Went That-a-Way: The Memoirs of a Western Film Director*, by Harry L. Fraser; edited by Wheeler Winston Dixon and Audrey Brown Fraser. 1990
23. *Order in the Universe: The Films of John Carpenter*, by Robert C. Cumbow. 1990
24. *The Films of Freddie Francis*, by Wheeler Winston Dixon. 1991
25. *Hollywood Be Thy Name*, by William Bakewell. 1991
26. *The Charm of Evil: The Life and Films of Terence Fisher*, by Wheeler Winston Dixon. 1991

The Word Made Flesh

Catholicism and Conflict
in the Films of Martin Scorsese

by
Michael Bliss

Filmmakers, No. 45

The Scarecrow Press, Inc.
Lanham, Md., and London

SCARECROW PRESS, INC.

Published in the United States of America
by Scarecrow Press, Inc.
4720 Boston Way
Lanham, Maryland 20706

4 Pleydell Gardens, Folkestone
Kent CT20 2DN, England

British Cataloguing-in-Publication Information Available

Library of Congress Cataloging-in-Publication Data

Bliss, Michael. 1947– .
The word made flesh : Catholicism and conflict in the films of Martin Scorsese /
by Michael Bliss.
p. cm. — (Filmmakers; no. 45)
Includes index.
1. Scorsese, Martin—Criticism and interpretation. 2. Motion pictures—
Religious aspects—Catholic Church.
I. Title. II. Series : Filmmakers series; no. 45
PN1998.3 S39B65 1995 791.43'0233'092—dc20 95-1156 CIP

ISBN 0-8108-3019-1 (cloth : alk. paper)

Printed in the United States of America

⊖™ The paper used in this publication meets the minimum requirements of
American National Standard for Information Sciences—Permanence of
Paper for Printed Library Materials, ANSI Z39.48–1984.

DEDICATION

To Christina Banks, whose patient and tireless work on the manuscript as compositor, editor, proofreader, and all-around organizer made this book a reality.

The dual substance of Christ—the yearning so superhuman, of man to attain God . . . has always been a deep inscrutable mystery to me. My principal anguish and source of all my joys and sorrows from my youth onward has been the incessant, merciless battle between the spirit and the flesh . . . and my soul is the arena where these two armies have clashed and met.

—Nikos Kazantzakis, *The Last Temptation of Christ*

CONTENTS

INTRODUCTION

In a 1982 interview, Brian De Palma delivered what is probably an accurate assessment of Martin Scorsese's films when he said that "Marty's work will always be interesting because he has such a bizarre sensibility." Naturally, the terms that define this sensibility need to be adequately explored. Nevertheless, at the outset it may be instructive to examine what the general reactions to Scorsese's work are.

From seeing productions such as *Mean Streets*, *Taxi Driver*, *Raging Bull*, or *Cape Fear*, filmgoers might assume that Scorsese is a filmmaker overtly concerned with violence, yet such a conclusion overlooks the unusual tonal range of his films, from the urban tensions of *Who's That Knocking at My Door*, *Mean Streets*, *Taxi Driver*, and *The King of Comedy*; to the rebellious proletarian mood of *Boxcar Bertha* and the essentially humanistic themes explored in *Alice Doesn't Live Here Anymore*; to the contemplative atmosphere of *The Last Waltz* and the melancholy feelings engendered by *New York, New York* and *The Age of Innocence*.

Actually, most of Scorsese's work does not depict explicit violence at all. *The Last Waltz*, *New York, New York*, and *The Age of Innocence* contain no violent confrontations. *Knocking* contains only the non-contact gang fight and the fragmented rape scene memory sequence; while the violence in *Mean Streets*, *Alice*, *Taxi Driver*, and *King of Comedy* is carefully counterbalanced by sequences involving comedy and camaraderie. Only *Raging Bull*, unique among Scorsese's films, places physical confrontation at the film's thematic center. Yet even here, the emphasis on brutality is ostensibly the result of the anti-violence didactic intention that the director apparently had in mind.

What seems most disturbing about the violence in Scorsese's films is not only its immediacy but the implied forms that it takes, usually in the persons of characters who, while not acting violently, nevertheless seem to embody extremely aggressive tendencies. Much of Scorsese's cinematic violence results from the almost impossible demands that a society which views itself as orderly and organized

ix

imposes on individuals who, through socialization, are expected to suppress hostile tendencies in favor of correct and polite responses.

For many of Scorsese's protagonists, though, successful socialization has simply not taken place. As a consequence, aberrants such as Johnny Boy, Travis Bickle, and Jake La Motta make a living by harnessing their hostile or aggressive tendencies. Johnny Boy exists by dangerously juggling the demands of the various people to whom he owes money. Travis recklessly confronts his hatred of blacks and minorities by using his cab to pick up anyone, anywhere. Jake, more animal than man (although *Raging Bull*'s end attempts to contradict this view), seems suited for little other than fighting. Like Johnny Boy, Travis, and *King of Comedy*'s Rupert Pupkin (who only achieves fame through excessive means), La Motta is an outcast and a loner; and since these characters' interactions with other people are limited, they are free to pursue their unusual, untested ideas.

The result of these characters' socially dysfunctional status is violence—a violence, however, that presages readjustment. Charlie and Johnny Boy's shooting at *Mean Streets*' end teaches them a cruel lesson; the same may be said of Alice Hyatt (who learns a great deal about trust at the hands of Harvey Keitel's Ben) and of Jake (at least, we are expected to feel that Jake's incarceration initiates his moral recovery). What can we conclude, then, but that violence is meant to act as a redemptive force in these films, not only alleviating socially induced tensions (this effect is especially present in Rupert's case) but also acting as a cohesive agent that re-integrates the aberrant individual?

In Scorsese's canon, only *Who's That Knocking at My Door* and *Cape Fear* show us characters for whom self-recognition is not offered as a necessary corollary to violence. *Knocking*'s J.R. is still a lonely man at the film's end; unable to resolve his problems with "the girl," he is left isolated and miserable. *Cape Fear*'s Max Cady remains true to his violent credo right up to the moment of his death. With the exception of these films (and, as I argue in a later chapter, *Raging Bull*), this pattern of violence followed by enlightenment (even if the violence is of an interior kind, as in *The Age of Innocence*) continually reasserts itself, a horrifying situation since it makes violence a necessary prerequisite to self-awareness. Moreover, given the depicted regenerative capabilities of violence, we may infer that it is thereby not only an essential part of existence but one that, through its curative powers, affirms society's basic healthiness—that it is, in effect, a sane response to conditions that are quite often offensive or intolerable.

As a consequence, the violent individual, unfettered by restrictions on his behavior, becomes a lone avenger for justice, a cowboy affirming his right to bear arms. It must be noted that in many of these films (*Knocking*, *Boxcar Bertha*, *Mean Streets*), weapons are readily available despite the legal restrictions placed on their possession. To take the prime example: not only does *Taxi Driver*'s Travis Bickle find it quite easy to purchase any gun (or drug for that matter) that he cares to, but he is seen practicing his marksmanship skills in a shooting gallery that uses the kinds of targets employed on police academy firing ranges. The suggestion here is shocking: by virtue of his actions, Travis invites comparison with the police, another armed segment of society which, like him, sees its mission as one of patrolling and cleaning up the crime-infested city. The manner in which the film suggests by implication that the police are as aberrant as Travis (and vice versa) produces a view of a society totally out of control and headed, if we are to judge by the film's indecisive cataclysm, towards some vague, apocalyptic end.

While only separable from social-dysfunctional violence in a conceptual way, the erotic violence in Scorsese's films is nevertheless such a characteristic and powerful force that it deserves individual attention. Erotic violence in these films is that violence, either actual or implied, that arises out of sexual relationships. In its most restrained form it consists of jousts for control within heterosexual relationships. Erotic violence is present in J.R.'s refusal of the girl's tendered affection (an act that thereby establishes him as the relationship's dominant partner); in Alice's husband's insistent demands at the dinner table and his initial refusal to make love to her; in the power plays (most notably the argument about who "counts down the band") between Jimmy and Francine (power plays that re-surface in the love/ hate relationship between *King of Comedy*'s Rupert and Masha); and in the constant bickering between Jake and each of his two wives in *Raging Bull* and between the Bowdens in *Cape Fear*.

The most notable exception to the prevalence of this characteristic is in *Boxcar Bertha*. The relationship between Bertha and Bill is strikingly balanced. It is only when Bertha is involved with other men that jockeying for dominance (always practiced by the men, not Bertha) asserts itself. The conclusion here is obvious: it is traditional, male-oriented capitalist politics that creates and sustains antagonisms among people; aggression between sexual partners is a microcosmic repetition of hostilities between entrepreneurs and workers. *Boxcar*

Bertha's gang, though, is notably egalitarian; it contains a woman, a black, and a Jew as equal partners, and thereby gives us a view of an egalitarian society that would be possible if robber barons like Sartoris, who exploit the poor and powerless, were ejected from the country.

We are thus led to conclude that sexual inequality, and thereby inequality with respect to position or power, is a necessary outgrowth of the country's political inequality. As a consequence, the erotic violence in Scorsese's films—the rape scenes (*Knocking*), the scenes of assault against women (*Boxcar Bertha, Alice, Raging Bull, King of Comedy, Cape Fear*), the scenes depicting oppression of females (Iris in *Taxi Driver*)—can be viewed as integral reflections of American society.

The anger and violence directed against women in these films is an extension of the anger and violence that the films' male protagonists feel against society as a whole, whose oppression is so anonymous that it is virtually impossible to rebel against it. As a result, these men take out their frustrations against the most accessible and available target, the enemy whose obvious sexual difference brands them as a force that both attracts and repels: women.

Nor does it matter whether women are viewed as either virgins ("the girl" at *Knocking*'s beginning; Betsy when we first see her in *Taxi Driver*; Masha early in *The King of Comedy*; the nonetheless precocious Danielle of *Cape Fear*) or whores ("the girl" at *Knocking*'s end; Betsy after her break-up with Travis; Masha during her seduction of Jerry). *Taxi Driver* even gives us a character who occupies both worlds. Iris, while clearly a whore, exhibits in Travis's eyes such a potential for redemption that he works to restore her to her original state of virginity. The cruel black joke irony of *Taxi Driver*'s end is that this recovery is allowed to symbolically take place, as though only through Travis's murderous activities could Iris have been pried loose from Sport's clutches (when in fact, Iris previously indicated a willingness to leave the city and live on a commune, that is if Travis would accompany her).

These polarized views of women are, naturally, those of Scorsese's characters, whose sensibilities color most of what these films show us. In the typical Scorsese protagonist's view, everything is exaggerated: people are either friends or enemies; politics is either good or bad; success is either completely unattainable (e.g., Jake La Motta's lament that he'll never be able to fight Joe Louis, "the best there is") or just barely out of reach. The characteristic forms that these Manichean conceptions take are examined in the chapters on the individual films.

The meanings of Scorsese's films do not reside predominantly in the director's use of blatant cinematic technique. One would be hard pressed to find in Scorsese's work many examples of symbolic framing or allusive camera movement. Instead, Scorsese's most striking films (*Knocking*, *Mean Streets*, *Taxi Driver*, *Cape Fear*, *The Last Temptation of Christ*, *GoodFellas*) leave the viewer with the sensation of having been exposed to a unique milieu that serves as the overall communicator of the films' meanings.

We thus return to De Palma's observation about Scorsese's cinematic sensibility. Although Scorsese's work is extraordinarily rich in symbol and structure, we are initially impressed in a Scorsese film by two things: the acting and the script. The two actors who figure most prominently in Scorsese's films are Harvey Keitel (*Knocking*, *Mean Streets*, *Alice*, *Taxi Driver*, *The Last Temptation of Christ*) and Robert De Niro (*Mean Streets*, *Taxi Driver*, *New York, New York*, *Raging Bull*, *The King of Comedy*, and *Cape Fear*). Initially, both actors might seem to be exhibiting characterizations dictated by the scripts and suggested by the director. Yet a glance at some of the important work of Keitel and De Niro for other directors (Keitel in James Toback's *Fingers*, Ridley Scott's *The Duelists* and *Thelma and Louise*, and Nicolas Roeg's *Bad Timing*; De Niro in De Palma's *Greetings* and *Hi, Mom*, Coppola's *The Godfather Part II*, Kazan's *The Last Tycoon*, and Grosbard's *True Confessions*) should indicate that both actors' mannerisms appear so consistent and firmly fixed that we must assume that Scorsese merely drew upon Keitel and De Niro's ability to project menace and elicit sympathy at the same time.

Much has been made of Scorsese's association with scriptwriter Paul Schrader, who scripted *Taxi Driver* and *Last Temptation* and helped in rewriting Mardik Martin's script for *Raging Bull*. However, there is a subtle but significant distinction between Schrader's view of violence as a necessary part of some great schema and Scorsese's view that violence is an integrated form of behavior which seems to be a part of regular existence. In essence, Schrader makes of violence a religious artifact, part of a ceremony whose expected outcome is redemption. For Scorsese, violence—although it may lead to some change in a character—is not a tool to be exploited, but merely a normal part of life.

Moreover, in Schrader's universe there is virtually no room for humor, even of the dark variety. Only *Taxi Driver* and *Last Temptation* exhibit a dark humor, a characteristic very possibly introduced into the films by the director since Schrader's own films do not contain humor, only small bits of comic relief as though it were an expected device tossed in solely for its entertainment value.

In Scorsese's work, though, violence and comedy are linked in frightening juxtapositions. The bad joke gun-taunting in *Knocking*, the robbery highjinks in *Boxcar Bertha*, the pool room fight and Charlie's pretend shooting of Teresa in *Mean Streets*, Travis's ridiculing of the Secret Service agent in *Taxi Driver* (which reveals his potential for controlled violence), the abduction of Jerry Langford in *The King of Comedy*, the death and escapes in *After Hours*—all of these events, excessive though they may be, have their impact perceptibly altered by the humor that characterizes them. In essence, by juxtaposing violence (either real or implied) and comedy, Scorsese implicitly ridicules exaggerated actions, although he notably complicates this schema by continuing to depict violence as a prelude to the attainment of the qualities that his characters desire: a modicum of peace (*Taxi Driver*), self-consciousness (*Mean Streets, Raging Bull*), fame (*King of Comedy*), or self-justification (*Cape Fear*).

I like to refer to Scorsese as the poet of violence because of the way that he stylizes exaggerated behavior in his films. It should be understood here that I am not talking about the kind of representation of killing exemplified in the work of Sam Peckinpah. Peckinpah's slow motion depiction of violence represents an attempt to reveal what the director sees as the balletic grace inherent in it. In contrast, even when he employs slow motion, Scorsese sees nothing romantic about violence. Thus, when Gaga is threatened with a gun during one of *Knocking*'s party sequences, the scene's slow motion only compounds the terror. The slow motion backward track away from *Taxi Driver*'s final blowout increases the horror by allowing time for a more extended audience reaction; in *The King of Comedy*, Rupert's time-expanded move through the crowd towards Jerry Langford produces an appreciable uneasiness resulting, in part, from the sequence's protraction.

Characters in Scorsese's films often seem to derive their most attractive qualities from a font of near-violent, aggressive behavior that is represented as an integral part of their personalities; thus, the volatile temper of men like J.R., Charlie, Johnny Boy, Travis, Jimmy, Jake, and Rupert both motivates them in playful moments and fuels their violent outbursts.

The aforementioned traits are significant, and form the basis of Scorsese's early filmmaking. What concerns me now, though, is the director's progress towards a mature vision. That vision is present in the early films, but we see it reach a new (albeit problematical) assuredness in Scorsese's more recent films.

The most notable characteristic of Scorsese's films derives from what I refer to as the director's Catholic sensibility. Scorsese is indebted to Catholicism for suggesting the manner in which his characters attempt to resolve the opposition between the word and the flesh, between the behests of Catholicism as derived from the Bible and the rigorous demands of living in the world and dealing with all of its nagging adjustments, deceits, and compromises.

The implicit notion here is that all of Scorsese's characters are in one sense or another moralists. In early films such as *Who's That Knocking at My Door* and *Mean Streets*, we can see that the world in which the characters exist is one in which the manifest presence of God has been either withdrawn or was never present to begin with. There is no support in the material world for the religious obsession with which Scorsese's characters find themselves involved. Indeed, events do very little to aid these characters in their quests for a productive life or some sort of moral absolution.

In fact, it doesn't even matter if the characters are in the real world, as is Alice in *Alice Doesn't Live Here Anymore*, or are in some form of hell, as is Travis in *Taxi Driver*. What they're still searching for is some way to put into practice the behests that the god with whom they are in touch whispers in their ears. In one way or another, then, these characters are all religious fanatics, that is, if by the term fanatic we mean someone who believes that God has spoken to them. Yet much of the time, like Jesus in *The Last Temptation of Christ*, these characters don't want the religious burden that has been thrust upon them.

The universe in which Scorsese's films take place is an unrelenting and, usually, unforgiving one. There are no compromises involved, and very little respite from pain. Telling virtually the same story from film to film, Scorsese tracks the map of his repeated concern with the question of how one can act morally in a morally skewed universe. From the slippage between these two realms emerges his characters' problems and, occasionally, their triumphs.

It is Scorsese's blessing to have a predilection for the kind of stories in which characters are caught up in the conflict between externally imposed values and their own natural desires. But when the director makes the mistake of choosing a story like *The Color of Money*, in which the tension generated between Eddie Felson's past successes and present moral impoverishment is, at best, rudimentary, his filmmaking becomes unconvincing simply because it is based on no credible conflict in the central character's personality.

Throughout his career, though, Scorsese has predominantly remained true to the main theme of the conflict between the temporal and religious realms. His insight into the anxieties of growing up as an Italian-American Catholic has always been firmly rooted in his own personal experience. Indeed, this conflict goes back to the first screenplay that Scorsese wrote, *Jerusalem, Jerusalem*, which was meant to be part one of a trilogy of films (the second and third of which are *Who's That Knocking at My Door* and *Mean Streets*) about the Italian-American experience in New York.[1]

The plot of *Jerusalem, Jerusalem*, portions of which emerge in *Who's That Knocking at My Door* and *Mean Streets*, deals with J.R., who through a series of actions is compelled to see the difficulty of reconciling the demands of Catholicism with those of the flesh. The film was never made, Scorsese commenting that nobody would want to see a depressing film about religion, but the significance of the theme in Scorsese's work is enduring. That the film's theme goes back as far as St. Paul and St. Thomas does not detract from Scorsese's achievement in using it; indeed, if anything, it is a testimonial to the theme's enduring significance. It's to Scorsese's credit that he manages to successfully transpose the theme to the milieu of the lower East Side and then, in later films, to the world in general.

In *Boxcar Bertha*, we see the conflict between what is deemed right and what actually exists in the film's Marxist bias in favor of the rights of the individual worker as opposed to those of the bosses. It's therefore no surprise that in the film two characters are brought into conflict, both of whom are associated with Catholicism: the bible-quoting Sartoris (John Carradine) and the religiously-oriented Bill Shelley (David Carradine), who in appropriate religious symbology is crucified at the film's end (the two characters can almost be read as God the father and God the son; interestingly, they are played by a real life father and son).

Scorsese may denigrate this structure in his first pitch for commercial acceptance, *Alice Doesn't Live Here Anymore*, in which the conflict assumes the pedestrian form of the clash between Alice's desires to live out her dream and her ultimate acceptance of the reality of her needing a traditional relationship in which she is once more (despite the patina of independence that the film grants her) subserving herself to a man. However, the structure resurfaces strongly in *Taxi Driver*, in which Travis Bickle's inability to reconcile his desire for a traditional relationship with his socially unacceptable behavior dooms him to failure in any realm other than a violent one. One can profitably view Travis as a misinformed Jesus bearing not an olive branch but a sword and wreaking havoc in a despoiled marketplace. Conflicts like these are present in each successive Scorsese film right through *The Age of Innocence*, whose protagonist is torn between his devotion to the behavior that society condones and the promptings of his innermost desires.

In all, Scorsese warrants our attention for his dedication to his craft, for the perceptive messages about human relations and their curious mixture of tenderness and aggression, and for his admirable penchant for experimenting with different genres (drama, musical, comedy, documentary). If only for the reason that he has yet to receive the kind of detailed treatment that his work deserves, a book such as this one would be warranted. The fact that he is considered one of our most important living filmmakers makes such a study virtually imperative.

This book contains writing that spans a period of nine years, from revisions of chapters that originally appeared in *Martin Scorsese and Michael Cimino* through the ones in the present volume that begin with *After Hours*. One may note an alteration in my approach to Scorsese's films. The microanalysis of individual narrative elements has given way to a more thematically-based discussion of the films. This change is a result of two tendencies: a shift in my writing style and what I perceive as a change in the director's approach to his work. Predominantly, Scorsese is now more interested in telling stories than in creating devices to tell stories; thus the emphasis in Scorsese's recent films is more on theme and character than on symbols and allusions. In what I hope will be perceived as an economy of expression, this book's later chapters reflect this shift in emphasis.

NOTES

1. Information on this film is from Mary Pat Kelly's book *Martin Scorsese: The First Decade* (New York: Redgrave Publishing Co., 1980), pp. 42-56.

Chapter One

LET ME IN; LET ME OUT

As a debut feature film, *Who's That Knocking at My Door* (1969) is a remarkable achievement. Shot in black-and-white on a low budget, the film emerges as not only an important work that comments on male bonding and the influences of religion on Italian-Americans, but also as a striking precursor of most of Scorsese's future work. *Knocking* contains virtually all of the major themes that are prevalent in later Scorsese films: the insular integrity of the Italian-American community; the difficulty of establishing an extended relationship with a member of the opposite sex; the anxieties of urban life; and the yearning for union with kindred spirits (always male) as opposed to the desires of the flesh for sexual satisfaction. The latter tendency subjects *Knocking*'s (and, later, *Mean Streets*'s) characters to the stresses to which Italian-American Catholics are exposed as a result of an upbringing that condemns their physical desires without making available to them anything other than the most enervated alternative to these problems: the supposed solace of the church, which Scorsese shows is unequal to the task of providing spiritual or physical comfort.

Knocking's action begins in a shabby tenement apartment, where a grandmotherly woman[1] is preparing a bread-like pastry. While the soundtrack incessantly hammers out a series of noises that sound like some grinding, insistent machinery at work, the woman prepares, kneads, and shapes the dough, and then bakes it. Then, after a short dissolve, she distributes the cake to four young children.

Throughout the scene we are given indications of just how pervasive the religious influence is going to be in this film. We pass from a close-up of a votive candle in the apartment to shots of a statue of the Virgin Mary. These latter shots dissolve into a view of the elderly woman, suggesting a relationship between the two figures, the one Jesus' mother, the second the maternal moving force behind what

1

we must, given the scene's ecclesiastical trappings, view as a religiously-tinged breaking and distributing of the loaves among the faithful.   Indeed, throughout the eating scene Scorsese places the camera in a position from which the Virgin's statue is either glimpsed in the background or situated in the foreground; in the latter case, the Virgin appears to be looking down on, and perhaps approving of, the communal sharing of food that is taking place here.

The implications of this short scene are striking: the old woman assumes the role of the elder, the progenitor of the tribe, supposedly imbued with wisdom and grace; the young children who eat the bread are the congregation or disciples. The bread-breaking, then, symbolizes the passing on of religion and knowledge to the next generation.

What this religion and knowledge yield, and what the next generation is up to, are made clear in *Knocking*'s next shot as we see two of the film's principals, Joey (Lennard Kuras) and J.R. (Harvey Keitel), preparing for a street fight with a Puerto Rican opponent who kisses his crucifix before beginning the altercation. Thus far, then, the results of religion are violence, not peace.

Scorsese then cuts from the street fight (glimpsed only briefly) to a shot of a butcher chopping meat. The butcher's dividing of the meat into sections with his cleaver invites comparison between his activities and those of the old woman, who cuts the bread with a knife. The fact that the grandmother and butcher sequences bracket the street fight further suggests that the street scene's symbolic action is somehow "enclosed" by these two figuratively rich activities.

Both the old woman and butcher sequences involve food and the dividing of edibles for consumption. The meat-chopping scene implies that instead of the bread of life being divided, what we witness in Little Italy's streets is the actual stuff of life—raw, human meat, as in the street knife fight—being chopped up. The woman and the butcher are emblems of life in New York's Italian community; the activities of each, despite the ideas with which we would normally associate them (the woman as protector, the butcher as friendly merchant), represent a feeding of the spirit that allows the continued existence of destructive impulses. Ironically, while the bread-breaking scene would traditionally connote the distribution of peace and satisfaction, it here suggests just the opposite: the passing on as a heritage of a violence akin to that perpetrated on animals who, like the street-fighting youths, are routinely slaughtered. Even at this early point in *Knocking*, we see that conflict, not harmony, is going to be the reigning force in this film universe.[2]

J.R. and Joey are next seen walking down a street and entering Joey's establishment, the 8th Ward Pleasure Club, where their mutual friend Sally Gaga (Michael Scala) is playing poker. Gaga is in debt to Joey, and is thus strictly speaking gambling with some of Joey's money. Joey therefore breaks up the game by slapping Gaga around. The youngster apologizes, but Joey replies, "Your priest you say you're sorry to," suggesting thereby that confession is cheap, and that what counts is not the spiritual coin (in this case, penance) in which the church deals but the concrete and material things in life, such as the money that Gaga owes Joey.[3]

In the aftermath of this clash we are given glimpses into J.R.'s mind that introduce one of the film's main concerns: the relationship between J.R. and a female character referred to in the credits as "the girl" (Zina Bethune). In this early flashback scene between the two characters, J.R. and the girl are seen sitting on the wooden benches of the Staten Island ferry sitting room, where they are waiting for the ferry back to New York. The girl is reading a magazine, occasionally sniffling into a handkerchief; J.R., carrying a parcel (containing the stuff-of-death bread; he mentions having visited his mother), is drawn to a magazine photo of John Wayne, at which he keeps staring. The girl notes his attentiveness; consequently, their conversation at first centers on the film from which the photo is culled: John Ford's *The Searchers*.[4]

Although the conversation between J.R. and the girl initially seems innocent and sweet, Scorsese works assiduously to undermine what appears to be the essential purity of their blossoming relationship. The conversational opener about *The Searchers* may seem a relatively benign way to begin talking until one recalls Wayne's attitude towards the only female character from *The Searchers* whom J.R. mentions: Natalie Wood's Debbie Edwards.

In the Ford film, Wayne's Ethan Edwards clearly hates the mature Debbie, whom he views as sullied because she has lived with (and, the suggestion is made, had sex with) the Indians who kidnapped her. Additionally, in mentioning *The Searchers'* Martin Pawley (Jeffrey Hunter), J.R. brings in by allusion the polarized attitudes towards women that he himself will exhibit. Like Hunter's Martin, J.R. believes in female purity: Martin appreciates the innocence of Vera Miles's Laurie Jorgensen, and even seems to think that the grown-up Debbie still enjoys the same quality. Yet like Ethan, who believes in Debbie's corruption (although he does keep his promise to bring her back home), J.R. also realizes how easily women can be debased. As we shall see, throughout *Knocking* J.R. swings wildly between these two attitudes in his behavior towards the girl. This essentially unrealistic, polarized view of women—which divides them into two classes, the redeemed and the damned, the virgins and the whores—reflects the church-influenced attitude towards existence that, along with other elements of their Catholic upbringing, poisons the minds and lives of *Knocking*'s male characters, all of whom are trapped by their world view.

While the conversation between J.R. and the girl continues, Scorsese undermines our sense of time and our desire to wish J.R. and the girl well by cutting back to the present. No sooner does the scene of J.R. and the girl talking on the ferry end than we see Joey (in the present) closing the pleasure club's padlock (an action depicted in giant close-up), then J.R. buttoning his overcoat and slamming closed the door of Joey's car. While these three shots may be regarded as merely advancing the film's action, they can also—given *Knocking*'s emblematic bent—be read as symbols of the claustrophobic, insular attitude towards life that J.R., Joey, and Sally Gaga all share. Locked up, buttoned into, shut inside their religiously polluted view of life, the three friends are trapped in an existence within which they find reaching out and establishing a forthright relationship with a woman to be simply impossible.

With the next scene, in Joey's car, the conversation has somehow turned to the topic of women. J.R. tells Joey, "I'd like to see you get a girl without paying five dollars for her." Joey assures J.R. that he can, but Scorsese quickly contradicts this assertion. Instead, we see the third representative of the trio, Sally Gaga, back at the club, kissing a young woman who later complains that forty dollars is missing from her purse. In flashback, we see that Gaga stole the money from her while they were kissing. The woman complains that she can't get home without money, so Sally separates a bill from his pocket and gives it to her for cabfare. Significantly, it is a five dollar note. As Gaga's example makes clear, none of the friends gets something for nothing; indeed, the spiritual price that J.R. is to pay for his association with "the girl" is considerable.

J.R., Joey, and Gaga are next seen riding up in a garage elevator. The lift's machinery gives out a harsh, annoying, grinding noise similar to the noise on the soundtrack during the bread-baking and breaking sequence, thus reminding us of the cruel religious mechanism that keeps these characters trapped in their lives. Scorsese then employs an implied match-cut: the upward-moving elevator leads us to anticipate a later scene in a high place; Scorsese satisfies this expectation by showing us J.R. and the girl on a roof during daytime, where J.R. is holding forth about Lee Marvin's nastiness in *The Man Who Shot Liberty Valance*, a film in which, significantly, Marvin's Liberty Valance threatens the identity of Jimmy Stewart's naive tenderfoot, Ransom Stoddard. Again, then, as in the reference to *The Searchers*, we are exposed to a film character who represents a point of view which, if adopted, could sabotage a young man's social and sexual development. It is difficult to avoid the conclusion that J.R. is obsessed with these cinematic characters because he himself feels somehow threatened, and that the person who threatens him is, ironically, the girl.

Scorsese then cuts back to the elevator sequence (the rooftop episode with the girl, as is true of all of her appearances in the film until its end, has been a flashback memory), with J.R. and Joey staring at the elevator shaft's blank wall from their extremely limited environs, and then back again to a shot of the club, which is littered with filled ashtrays and dirty dishes, within which Gaga has just stolen the aforementioned forty dollars. The effect of these scenes is blatant: there is no escape from the confines of one's crude existence; love, when it occurs at all, takes place in grimy, unattractive surroundings (the dirty club; during the love scene between J.R. and the girl, street noises continually intrude). In any case, love never affords a release from one's trapped existence. Gaga is a compulsive thief, stealing even from someone with whom he is acting romantic (thus the harsh-sounding slammed door as Gaga's girlfriend walks out of the club figuratively shuts him into his destructive mode of behavior); and there is no reason to believe that either Joey or J.R. would be liberated from their own obsessive actions, regardless of their emotional attachments.

To affirm the sense of entrapment, Scorsese then returns us to still another enclosed place, this time the car again. The claustrophobia thus created is further accentuated by the repetition of action; the reversion to the car creates a sensation of dull, inescapable sameness. From the car interior shot, Scorsese cuts to a brief shot of J.R. and the girl on the roof, reminding us of two things: the unrealized possibility of open spaces (even up on the roof, the couple seem hemmed in by the

surrounding buildings) and the fact that although what we are
witnessing is a developing mutual affection, in truth the relationship is
already over. All we see until the very end of *Knocking* are J.R.'s
memories of the girl; throughout the majority of the film, the
relationship is a *fait accompli* locked inside J.R.'s mind.

The following shot once again returns us to the car, whose
destination is either indeterminate ("Where should we go tonight?"
"Uptown." "How about the village?" "I want to go uptown.") or
annoyingly repetitious (back to the dead-end destination of the club).
It is to the latter place that J.R., Joey, and Gaga are now headed. No
sooner do they arrive than entrapment once again sets in. Joey says,
"Close the [car] windows," and we are given tight close-up shots of the
electric windows shutting. Then the car doors are slammed, the club
is opened (an action that leads the three principals back into a confined
space), and we are given three successive shots of closure: a car
window closing again (another throwback in time, further frustrating
our desire for progress) and two identical shots of the club door
closing.

With such a depressing mood thus created, we are prepared
for a return to the past tense and another memory scene between J.R.
and the girl. This time they are in the bedroom of J.R.'s mother's
apartment. It is in this sequence that one can for the first time fully
appreciate Scorsese's choice of Bethune for the character of "the girl."

Although *Knocking* is shot in black-and-white, one can see that
in the film Bethune is a blonde; if anything, her blondness is more
striking in black-and-white given the film stock's greater contrast
possibilities over color. The girl's long straight hair is attractive; she
appears quite beautiful and pristine—meek, shy, polite.

Appropriately, the girl in this scene is quite a complement to
the religious artifacts (which traditionally, along with other associ-
ations, connote purity) that are scattered throughout the room. There
is a crucifix over the bed; a statue of the Virgin stands on the bureau.
The scene is not without its worldly taint, though, since throughout it,
street sounds reminding us of the Catholic-influenced but nonetheless
corrupt milieu in which the film takes place can easily be heard.

As a result of his upbringing, which apparently taught him that
good girls don't engage in sex,[5] J.R. feels reluctant to make love to the
girl. Although she seems perfectly (one might say innocently) willing,
and we see that her skirt being brushed up and her breasts being
caressed elicit no objections from her, J.R. cannot go through with it.

During the sequence the following exchange takes place:

J.R.:   I love you, but . . .
The girl: What is it?

Scorsese then provides the visual answer: we are given a mirror shot that shows the statue of the Virgin on the bureau. "It" is religion, the Catholic attitude towards sex that unrealistically divides people into two mutually exclusive categories (sinners and saints), thereby making it impossible for J.R. to accept this woman's love. In essence, J.R. himself is the mirror image of the statue Virgin; unyielding, always watching, always judging, he is never seen participating in and sharing the very human love that all of the film's characters need.

Of course, the situation here is wildly paradoxical. J.R.'s apparently sincere love for the girl cannot be expressed physically. As we see later, though, J.R. has absolutely no trouble making love to women about whom he doesn't care: the prostitutes whom he frequents.

J.R. finds it impossible to realize the truth of his situation. His explanation of why he cannot make love to the girl falls as far short of satisfaction as the church's unrealistic injunction to either "marry or burn." J.R. states, "Just not now—old-fashioned—call it anything you want—I love you first—as you—to me—if you love me you'll understand what I mean."

We are immediately given a contrast to this scene's seriousness in the following sequence, which depicts a party. Significantly, where J.R. in the company of a romantically-associated woman was quite moody and withdrawn, in the party sequence, among his male friends, he is happy and jovial again. The party's frivolity, though, is purchased at a rather high price, since its main source of entertainment is a scene between Gaga and a gun-wielding young man who, after pointing his weapon at everyone in the room (with resultant laughs from all concerned), grabs Gaga around the neck and repeatedly thrusts the gun against his temple as though he were going to shoot him. The sequence is shot in slow motion and is accompanied on the soundtrack by the insistent refrain from the rock song "Watusi,"[6] lending an anxious sameness to the scene. Moreover, the slow motion not only draws out the horrifying action but also subtly duplicates the slightly torpid, drunken state of the party-goers, while throughout, the song repeats over and over.

Complementing this sense of entrapped repetition is Scorsese's use of repeated 360-degree pans during the scene, with each dissolving effortlessly, almost dreamily, into the next. The gun, and its eventual discharge (a bottle is shot off the kitchen table), is, given the sequence's juxtaposition with the bedroom scene in J.R.'s home, an obvious substitute for the potency (suggested by the hard metal gun) and ejaculation (the shot) that J.R. fails to achieve with his girlfriend. To heighten this contrast, in a reprise of the film's three-sequence opening, Scorsese once again employs a tripartite construction to communicate his film's meanings. First we have the scene with J.R. and the girl, then the party sequence. The third sequence brings us back to J.R. and the girl, thus suggesting that, as in previous sequences that doubled back on themselves, progress in *Knocking*'s universe (movement beyond one's limitations) is impossible. No sooner does the gunshot at the party sound than Scorsese transports us to the outside of a movie theater where, with repeated gunshots on the soundtrack, we are given successive stills of John Wayne in *Rio Bravo* and Dean Martin in *Scaramouche*, films in which both actors play potent gunmen whose firearms are emblems of their prowess.

As Junior Walker's "Shotgun" appropriately plays on the soundtrack, J.R. and the girl are seen leaving the theater while J.R. tells his date about the only kinds of women which he believes western movies dramatize.

> J.R.:   That girl [Angie Dickinson] in that
>   picture was a broad.
> The girl: What do you mean, a broad?

After an awkward pause, the girl finally states, rather uncertainly, "You don't mean that." Scorsese then concretizes J.R.'s response, choosing to let the visuals once again provide the answer. The immediately following scene shows J.R. in an empty, sterile, rundown loft, in the middle of which is situated a bed where he copulates with a number of women who, if we are to judge by their lurid attire and makeup and J.R.'s obvious willingness to frolic with them, would indeed qualify as (to use J.R.'s term) "broads" (or, to adopt a more potent and later-used term, whores). With The Doors' "The End" (a song about death and forbidden sex) playing on the soundtrack, the scene takes on a truly morbid quality. This sensation is affirmed when at one point J.R., standing over a reclining nude woman, spews a deck of cards over her body; the mock ejaculation only serves to heighten the scene's morbid tone.[7]

We then return to J.R. and the girl and J.R.'s fuller explanation of what a broad—like the women with whom we have just seen him—really is. "There are girls and then there are broads," he says.[8]

As though to suggest that there exists a possible alternative to the morbid male relationships that are all that J.R., Joey, and Gaga seem capable of, Scorsese's next scene shows us J.R., Joey, and an unnamed third young man in Joey's car as the young man ferries them to upstate New York. At first, it seems that perhaps in escaping from the city's confining and unproductive atmosphere something positive will occur. Gaga's replacement by an older male also hints that we may finally see J.R. and Joey acting maturely. Instead, the first thing that the three are seen doing upstate is sitting in a bar. The idea to do so is Joey's and the event's significance is clear: Joey is merely repeating what he does in his Manhattan pleasure club; it is as though he has never left home. The new male now says, "I want to show you something beautiful," but Joey quickly reduces this hopeful suggestion to the basest physical and sexual terms: "OK, what's her name?"

However, the young man does have his way, convincing Joey and J.R. to climb a mountain with him. At one point in the climb, Joey refuses to go on. Only J.R.'s goading (he implicitly affirms Joey's masculinity—but then only at someone else's expense, just as the gun-wielding man at the party did when he victimized Gaga—by saying to Joey, "Don't let this fag scare us; come on") induces Joey to continue. Ironically, it is fear of snakes, a traditional phallic symbol, that almost deters Joey, indicating that like J.R., he is probably incapable of dealing with sexuality in a direct and forthright way.

When they reach the mountain top, Joey fails to see the significance of the beautiful view. "So what's up here?" he asks. "Big deal." His last remark, though, is the most telling. "I don't understand," he says, and while this is probably true for him, we may wonder what J.R. is thinking as he thoughtfully gazes into the setting sun. Is he, in fact, on the verge of realizing what an orientation towards death and enclosure represents?

As in much else of *Knocking*, the answer is provided in visual form. J.R. and the girl are once again in J.R.'s mother's apartment; the girl lights a votive candle and places it on the table. "Now what are you doing with a holy candle on the table?" J.R. asks. Apparently, the girl does not conceive of religion as J.R. does; for her, religion is not so sacrosanct that it cannot be integrated along with normal daily activities. J.R., though—trapped at the level of the restrictive word (not the benevolent spirit) of Catholicism—cannot tolerate such behavior. Ironically, he is about to demonstrate that when it comes to an essential religious quality—compassion—he is incapable of expressing or understanding it.

The girl relates how she was raped by a former boyfriend. She describes the "boy" as always having been a perfect gentleman—that is, until the last fateful night. Thus, the boy, like J.R., exhibited two polarized, antithetical types of behavior: one sweet, kind, and basically asexual; one cold, ruthless, aggressive, and sexual. As with the conception of women held by J.R., there is no middle ground of perception or behavior for the film's men: a woman is either a virgin or a slut; a man either acts tenderly or as a beast.

With the soundtrack playing "Don't Ask Me to Be Lonely" (ironic in that both the past encounter with the boy and the present encounter with J.R. will leave the girl quite alone), the girl relates the rape. As the rape nears culmination, the images Scorsese gives us of it come faster and faster and the music on the soundtrack becomes first double, then triple-tracked, reflecting the growing confusion and anxiety of the scene as it is recalled. The fact that along with the rape scene (many of whose frozen memory images Scorsese presents in stills, and which ends when the boy is seen pulling up the girl's skirt, at which point she screams) Scorsese also inserts flash shots from J.R. and the girl's love scene here, suggests a tragic connection between the two relationships that in purely visual terms seems to doom the later one to failure.

In pitifully predictable fashion, J.R. is unable to accept the girl in what he obviously considers is her sullied state. Although the girl touchingly states that "with you it'll be the first time," J.R. cannot share this view. Having known her as essentially "chaste," J.R. cannot now accept her as sullied. Bluntly and viciously, he reacts.

> How can I believe you? How can I believe that
> story? It just doesn't make any sense. How do I
> know you didn't go through the same story with him?
> You go out with a guy and you don't even know
> what he's like?

The result is that the girl leaves; Scorsese gives us the shot of her slamming the apartment door three times. The number suggestively leads us into the next sequence, in which our three male principals, reunited, enter a bar and order three scotch and waters. Once again, we see J.R. gladly returning to the company of his male friends, displaying an ease of which he never seems capable when he is with the girl. The soundtrack cruelly rings with "ain't that just like me cracking up over you?" and on the repeated words "don't you want to love me, too?" the laughter from the bar blends into the screams emanating from the girl's mouth during the rape scene (which is again depicted in freeze frames), thus drawing a painful connection between the girl's past distress and J.R.'s present pleasure. It is almost as though the two qualities were reciprocal, and in a certain sense they are, since J.R.'s preference for homophilic over heterosexual love allows him to get along with his male friends while simultaneously making it impossible for him to consummate his relationship with the girl.

There is no doubt that J.R. misses the girl. Joey earlier accuses him of thinking about her, although J.R.'s hostile reaction to this remark suggests that he considers his yearning for her as a sign of weakness. Still, after the bar sequence, when J.R. is left alone in his apartment house lobby, drunk and tired, he reaches out his left hand for the girl and Scorsese intercuts a tender flashback shot of her, allowing J.R., at least in his memory, to caress her hair.

However, no sooner does this remembered lyricism end than J.R. is back with his friends, at another party in another woefully dingy apartment. This time, Gaga is deputized to bring back some women (as Joey puts it, "This is the party you promised us? Where are the broads?"). Two young women do eventually arrive (one of whom, like Joey, fears phallic things that crawl), although they aren't greeted with any notable graciousness. Eventually, J.R. breaks up the simultaneous make-out scenes and the girls depart screaming. Yet the manner in which Joey and J.R. laugh over this turn of events indicates that they derive more pleasure from each other's company than they do from associating with women.

Scorsese still provides J.R. with one more chance at a productive heterosexual relationship. Drunk and missing the girl (just as he was earlier in his hallway), he goes to the girl's apartment early one morning. At first, it seems that they may be reconciled. Then J.R. says, "I forgive you and I'm gonna marry you anyway." Probably the most painful word to the girl is "anyway," since her circumstances hardly merit a dismissal of this sort. What's more, J.R.'s statement seems to offer some sort of moral absolution, demonstrating that he is still trapped in his Catholic-infected mentality.

When his inappropriate offer is refused, J.R. becomes hostile, attempting with words to relegate the girl to Hell.

> You can't marry me anyway . . . if that's the kind of broad you are . . . who do you think you are, the Virgin Mary or something? Who else is gonna marry you, you whore?

J.R. refuses to be reasonable since, in his distorted view, to accept the girl as flawed would be tantamount to admitting that she was his equal, a situation that would entail his loss of power over her, something he could not tolerate. As he states, "you want me to crawl back to you." For J.R., he either has to walk tall like a great western hero or "crawl"; there is no middle ground of reasonable activity.

J.R. goes on to intimate that the girl somehow enticed him by letting him enter her apartment, and compounds his offense by again (as he did in the previous quotation) placing her in the category he reserves for fallen women. "Leading me on like that, letting me in here at this hour of the morning . . . what kind of *broad* does that make you?" (emphasis added).

Significantly, after being asked to leave the girl's apartment, J.R. goes to church. The girl, though, told J.R. to "go home." But for J.R., the church is home, an enclosed place where he may reaffirm his tragically limited perspective (Cf. Charlie's literal and figurative returns to the church in *Mean Streets*). We see J.R. enter the confessional (although exactly what he has to confess at this point is unclear, since he obviously feels that he has acted justly). Then, in a powerful montage sequence whose structure anticipates the end of *Mean Streets*, we see J.R. in the confessional, shots of statues of the Virgin, and numerous views of stigmata-adorned Christs. The juxtapositions are instructive. Immediately after J.R. enters the confession booth, we see a shot of J.R. kissing the girl in his apartment; a crucifix on the wall is in the background. Obviously, J.R.'s true confessor should be this sweet, devoted woman, but he's too strongly influenced by his homophilic obsession and his Catholic upbringing to be honest with her. We see J.R. leaving the confessional and then a shot of J.R. kissing the girl as church bells sound in the background, signaling the holy union, the desired wedding, that will never take place.

More shots of statues follow, with an especial concentration on their stigmata, followed by a shot of the girl's upper thigh as though, in J.R.'s tainted view, the vaginal opening is the ultimate wound, bleeding not salvation but corruption into the world.

A shot of the letters INRI follows, then the thigh again to underscore the point about stigmata. The bread-breaking scene then reappears, followed by the rape scene. The suggestion here is striking: the breaking of the bread, the passing on of the Catholic doctrine of polarized good and evil, not only signifies the sharing of a philosophy of death, but condemns one to a self-righteous, lonely, and violent existence.

The film's last scene gives us a mirror image of *Knocking*'s opening (which showed us Joey and J.R. walking down the street together); it depicts Joey and J.R. parting, moving into the shadows as the camera pulls back from the street, thereby declaring that all of these male characters are condemned to pass into the darkness of ignorance, isolation, and death. The soundtrack during the end credits may feature "I Love You So," but this song is clearly an ironic counterpoint to the film's message about the failure of love and compassion. At the end of *Who's That Knocking at My Door*, the film's opening symbols and allusions achieve their full resonance. The bread being broken is not the staff of life but the stuff of death, and the answer to the question posed by the film's title and the song that plays during the church montage sequence ("Who's That Knocking at My Door?") is clear: it is the Catholic-corrupted, Catholic-appropriated Jesus, the God of pain and destruction (thus the blood coming out of J.R.'s mouth after he kisses the dead God's feet) who is knocking at the door; it is the God of morbidity who demands entrance.

NOTES

1.   The film's credits identify this woman as "J.R.'s mother," as does a short allusive comment made later by J.R. Regardless of her actual identity, her function in the film as a matriarchal figure of the Italian community remains in force.

2.   It must be remembered, though, that what we are watching here is a stylized representation of the Italian-American heritage. The loving, supportive aspects of this lifestyle are communicated in Scorsese's short film *Italian American*, in which Scorsese's parents, Charles and Catherine (the latter appears not only in *Knocking* as the grandmother figure but also in *Mean Streets*, *King of Comedy*, and

GoodFellas), are featured. Of course, given any film's inevitable stylization, *Italian American*'s point of view is also necessarily limited and, to that extent, suspect.

3. The statement strongly anticipates what Charlie says to Johnny Boy in *Mean Streets* when the latter starts making excuses about why he hasn't made his weekly loan payment to Michael: "Michael doesn't care if you're depressed; what is he, your priest?"

4. The reference here to *The Searchers* anticipates Scorsese's use of a clip from the Ford film in *Mean Streets*. In both *Knocking* and *Mean Streets*, *The Searchers* is extracted to underscore the violent tendencies that are soon to surface in the film we are watching.

5. Some of the promotional ad slicks for *Knocking* quite successfully appropriated this theme. Alluding to J.R.'s obsession, one advertisement for the film stated, "You're a virgin or a broad; he wants a first-time girl."

6. In addition to establishing a milieu evoking the youth culture of the fifties and sixties, music in *Knocking* (and, as we shall see, in *Mean Streets* as well) plays an integral part in communicating the film's meanings. The hard-rocking sounds of "Ginny" provide an aural complement to the tumultuous street fight at the film's beginning. When J.R. and the girl meet on the roof, the soundtrack's "I've Had It," with its theme of disappointment in love, complements the scene's tragic ambiance. Music is only alluded to in J.R.'s question in the girl's apartment about her Percy Sledge record; Sledge's "When a Man Loves a Woman" represents the idealized version of what J.R. thinks he feels towards the girl. Part of the song's lyric ("When a man loves a woman, don't need no one else") is in sharp contrast to J.R.'s ever-present need for his male friends.

7. It is tempting to speculate that the Saigon hotel room sequence in Francis Coppola's *Apocalypse Now* (which is also orchestrated to "The End") derives much of its imagery and sense of insularity from this scene. A review of *Knocking* in the British Film Institute's *Monthly Film Bulletin* (43:512; September, 1976, p. 203) claims that this loft sequence is "a nude fantasy scene" which Scorsese added to *Knocking* in order "to increase the film's chances of distribution." Indeed, the film's credits list the sequence's female participants as "dream girls." The review's author, Tom Milne, goes on to assert that "this interpolation of an undoubted fantasy in a film which is already playing tentatively with time and memory, raises totally unnecessary doubts and hesitations . . . (whether, for instance, the perfectly straightforward flashback to the rape might not rather be J.R.'s fantasy—in which case the girl could be lying)."

Milne tends to miss the point here. Although he claims that the sequence's inclusion obscures the meaning of the forthcoming mountain-climbing scene, Milne fails to note that the "fantasy" sequence occurs, not immediately before the mountain-climbing scene but before a return to J.R. and the girl leaving the movie theater, where they have just seen *Rio Bravo* and *Scaramouche*. The mountain-climbing scene occurs *after* the second scene showing J.R. and the girl talking about these two films. Sandwiched as it is between two essentially same-time, same-place sequences involving J.R. (who is reacting to the films) telling the girl about the differences between "girls" and "broads," the loft sequence acts as a reinforcement and exemplification of the absurd distinction that J.R. insists on making.

Milne is correct when he claims that we may treat the loft sequence as a fantasy or dream, just as we may also treat the rape scene as unreal. But to worry about whether the scenes are "true" (as Milne does in suggesting that the girl might by "lying" to J.R.) is to raise an irrelevant issue. Real or not, these two sequences clearly belong to the speakers in each sequence's starting-off point: J.R. (outside the movie theater) in the earlier threesome, the girl in the three later related scenes (in which we see the girl and J.R. in the kitchen; the flashback occurs; then we are back in the kitchen). Whether these inserted sequences are "real" or not is beside the point. What counts here is that the character visually experiencing these scenes believes them to be true; thus, the scenes are accurate representations of each character's state of mind at the time. Moreover, the fact that these insertions fit exactly into the tripartite schema of assertion-exemplification-assertion that Scorsese has already established in *Knocking* (e.g., the bread baking/street fight-butcher/ bread baking opening; the can't-get-a-woman-without-paying-for-her/Gaga's theft/enclosure-elevator sequence; the elevator/ rooftop/return to elevator sequence, etc.) affirms their essential validity regardless of the scenes' "reality."

8.   J.R.'s Manichean view of women strongly anticipates the attitude evidenced by *Taxi Driver*'s Travis Bickle, for whom all women are either virgins or whores.

An earlier statement of J.R.'s makes the distinction he draws quite clear. "A broad isn't exactly a virgin. You play around with them; you don't marry them." In his ignorance, J.R. believes that by offering to marry this girl, whom someone has "play(ed) around with," he is doing her a favor.

Chapter Two

RADICALS ON THE RAILS

Boxcar Bertha (1972) is the earliest of the two films directed by Scorsese that center on a female protagonist, predating *Alice Doesn't Live Here Anymore* by two years. But while *Alice* leaves the viewer with a sense of fulfillment unachieved, *Boxcar Bertha* concentrates on a character who at the film's end has fully realized her aspirations. Like Alice, Bertha Thompson (Barbara Hershey) progresses from innocence to experience, but in the process, through affiliation with the labor movement and the oppressed proletariat, she achieves an identification with moral and spiritual forces that provide a more satisfying direction and structure to her life than anything that Alice Hyatt could ever hope to attain.

Boxcar Bertha gives us two characters to whom Bertha reacts: the head of the prosperous Reader Railroad, Sartoris, and her labor movement lover, Bill Shelley. In a sly bit of casting, Scorsese has these roles played by the father and son team of John and David Carradine.[1] Drawing on our simultaneous fascination with the elder Carradine's well-modulated voice and the inherently alienating upper-class bearing that he brings to the part (which is strongly at odds with the way that the workers with whom Bertha and Bill are allied comport themselves) as opposed to the young Carradine's unstylized actions and speech, Scorsese compels us, if only through the casting, to sympathize with the working-class characters that the film presents.

In fact, *Boxcar Bertha*'s beginning makes it virtually impossible for us to sympathize with any other group. What viewer would not be outraged by the manner in which the man in the film's opening sequence (who pays Bertha's father's wages) insists that Mr. Thompson return to the air in his faulty crop-dusting plane even though Mr. Thompson is warned by Bertha's mechanic companion, Von Morton, that the plane's engine is in poor condition? In essence, with the death of Mr. Thompson in a plane crash, the viewer's sympathies

16

are determined for the remainder of the film, as is Bertha's future, which is destined to have her side with the poor.

This distinction between the haves and the have nots, and the inherent injustice of the arrangement (a situation exacerbated by the Great Depression, during which the film takes place), determines *Boxcar Bertha*'s thematic course. The film is quite obviously partisan, somewhat unfairly stacking the deck against the rich (all of whom are depicted as greedy, smug, and—through the activities of their hired minions[2]—murderous), whereas the poor are seen as predominantly warm, accessible, and thereby attractive. In essence, *Boxcar Bertha* is a study in exaggerated contrasts.[3] Those with property or capital seem compelled to protect and increase their investments; in fact, we never see the rich doing anything other than attempting to make more money or discussing ways of doing so. The railroad owners, like Sartoris, who kill off union opponents in order to guard their property; the overfed, unctuous, high-rolling gambler (a man who is, significantly, accompanied by a railroad lawyer) who covets Bertha as though she were a piece of dry goods; even the madam[4] who sells her women like marketable commodities, and is always on the lookout for more salable items—all of these people's actions testify to the reprehensible behavior in which the rich will engage in order to remain rich. These well-to-do characters can be seen as perverted embodiments of the self-protective impulse, affirming through their actions the exploitative and morbid (by virtue of being blindly acquisitive and thereby death-oriented) essence of the capitalist system while doing things that they apparently view as nothing more than exercising their right to freedom of action.

Through the power of its images; through our appreciation of the loving relationship that even during the worst times remains strong for Bertha and Bill; through the endearing qualities of its supporting characters (Barry Primus's Rake Brown and Bernie Casey's Von Morton) and the engaging nature of its depression-era music,[5] *Boxcar Bertha* not only ably takes the populist, union side but successfully converts the viewer to its radical philosophy.

One can say that the film's entire thematic thrust is determined by the period in which it is situated, a time when the poor never seemed poorer, and the rich never seemed better off. Unfortunately, when Bertha, Bill, Von, and Rake band together and begin to steal from the organization that they have apparently identified as the most visible oppressor (the Reader Railroad), we cannot view their actions as those of spirited, fun-loving revolutionaries and progressives (although the robbery sequences usually produce pleasure, derived from seeing the railroad's money more equitably distributed). Rather, by deciding to express their opposition to the capitalist system through theft, the gang, by participating in the desire for wealth and by exposing themselves to the legal penalties that the system applies to its most visible opponents, have thereby been co-opted by capitalism in a way more insidious than they apparently realize.

Morbidly bent on acquiring the accoutrements of the rich (money and material goods), the gang turn into nothing more than cheap criminals. The implicit point is made by the union official to whom Bill gives some of the money he has stolen, when he tells Bill that the union's finances and activities must be above reproach if the organization is to be effective.

Thus, Bill is incorrect when (in response to Rake's reading out loud an article about them) he states, "I ain't a criminal; I'm a union man." Rake looks askance at him here, doubtless expressing the audience's suspicion that Bill is wrong; by this point he is indeed more thief than unionist.

Bill is the film's central political figure, a character whom we initially encounter speaking to a group of men near the train tracks, inspiring them with his rhetoric. Seeing him for the first time, Bertha immediately recognizes a kindred spirit in this man who talks about refusing to knuckle under to the power of the moneyed interests. Indeed, as Bertha probably realizes, it was her father's need for money to purchase food and clothing for his family that compelled him to go back up in his faulty plane. One should note, though, that after the crowd which Bill addresses is infiltrated by a couple of policemen and two of Sartoris's thugs, Bill quickly incites the gathered men to riot, not for any political purpose but merely to provide an escape for himself and Bertha, whom he grabs on his dash through the crowd.

Despite Bertha's assessment of him, Bill is correct when he claims that he is not really such a "straight shooter." Aside from the allusion to sexual penetration and ejaculation involved in the statement, if we take the reference as an evaluation of Bill's political activities, one must agree with his comment, since his motives in working for "the cause" are as self-serving as Sartoris's are in working to increase his wealth. Unlike the union official to whom he gives his three thousand dollars in stolen money, Bill is unable to see that the source of the funds is equally as important as the money itself, and that there is a necessity for capitalism's opponents to be honest if they are to effectively fight the prevailing social order.

Of course, in one sense this restriction on the actions of protesters is grossly unfair, since it compels the radicals and unionists to obey the law even while the powered elite, in the persons of their goon squads, can engage in murder, arson, and torture, secure in the knowledge that money will buy them protection from prosecution. For example, as *Boxcar Bertha* demonstrates, if a working men's insurrection occurs in the jail, why, even there, within a supposed stronghold of legality, murder may easily be done. In fact, it is the murderers who are seen in this part of the film to be the ones in command; Sartoris's thugs shoot to death a number of prisoners and then order the sheriff to clean up the mess that they tell him *he* has made.

Bill's character is redeemed through his affection for Bertha, whom he constantly tries to protect throughout the film. We may question Bill's becoming a robber (even if, in Robin Hood fashion, he channels the money back to the poor), but we must sympathize with his apolitical devotion to his lover. The irony here is that in a film whose basic concern appears to be depicting the inequities in the American capitalist system during the Depression, it is only the personal relationships that really seem to be worthwhile. We may admire Bill's gang's daring, but despite all of the rationalizing, the gang's actions are far from laudable.

This is not to imply that the gang willingly become thieves; they do not. In fact, the first robbery happens purely by chance. The train that the four friends stop is carrying money, but the gang doesn't know that when they hop aboard. It is only when the mail car attendant asks, "We get robbed?" that Bertha inquires, "Why, you got something to rob?" Only then does Von come up beside the railroad man and level his shotgun at him. Even at this point, it's clear that a robbery will not occur without the approval of all four friends, so Scorsese shows them voting. One by one they gesture with the tool appropriate in such an election: a gun. Bertha votes affirmatively by raising her gun. Rake, the man who formerly lived through deception (trying to pass as a Northerner), reluctantly joins in, having traded in his symbols of chance (the dice, which nonetheless turn against him) and forsaken his cards (which, when he plays, are always rigged, although he gets caught) for what he considers a more sure thing: a firearm. We have already seen Von vote. Finally, with great reluctance, Bill raises his pistol, and the gang's conversion to completely illegal means is complete.

The group has thus been changed into robbers (as opposed to the robber baron Sartoris, who makes money from the efforts of the working man) and has thereby passed beyond integrity into corruption, the corruption of money. This change is most evident later when Bertha and Rake visit Sartoris's party in order to rob him and his pompous, half-dead guests. The two are decked out as members of the upper class. Rake first appears, looking awkward and overdressed in a tuxedo, while Bertha is seen bedecked in a fancy gown (symbol of an upper-class allure to which she is unaccustomed, thus the poor fit of the dress on the proletarian-minded Bertha) and jewels appropriated in a previous train robbery. Nor are these trappings worn only to gain admittance to the party. Indeed, admission is secured by Von, who subdues the front-door guard with a rifle. The clothes' real purposes are two-fold: to flaunt affectation in the face of the guests as well as to gain pleasure from dressing up this way.

This latter characteristic is regrettable, since it tends to compromise the last remnant of the gang's integrity: their allegiance to the working class. The money that the gang secures through its robberies seems to morally degrade them. This effect is symbolized most strikingly in a later scene. We are already familiar with the affection that all of the friends have for each other; this emotion is tainted, though, as we see at one point when Bertha and Bill make love in the gang's hideout. The lovers sit on a red velvet cloth, perhaps stolen from one of Sartoris's plush club cars; Bertha's arms are garishly adorned with rings and bracelets culled from their previous robbery. The opulent jewelry seems not only misplaced but objectionable, symbols of a lifestyle which the film (in the persons of the wily Sartoris and his friends) encourages us to reject.[6]

From this point on, *Boxcar Bertha* becomes more and more violent as it moves towards some kind of tragic conclusion for Bertha and Bill's love. Rake is freed from the gang's increasing corruption through his shotgun death. Von also gains absolution through blood. Avenging Bill's crucifixion by shotgunning Bill's murderers to death, he emerges after the shooting spattered with blood, but at peace.

Significantly, Bertha and Bill do not engage in ritualistic bloodletting, although this does not mean that they will turn the other cheek when wronged. Nevertheless, in a film in which a great many people are killed—from squatters in tent cities, to poor men in jail, to the railroad thugs who kill Bill—it is important to note that not only are none of the murders committed by Bertha or Bill, but that neither of them ever attempts to use a gun (as Rake does before he is shot). Apparently, this reticent attitude towards violence is a screenwriter's ploy to keep the two characters sympathetic. The fact that Bertha never directly causes any violence (even when it might be warranted), while the only fight that Bill starts and in which he participates is against the businessman who hired Mr. Thompson, leads us to conclude that neither of them really has much of a taste for hostility.

The question remains: are Bertha and Bill, as the moral and intellectual leaders of the gang, suited to their revolutionary roles? One must conclude that they are not. We can only surmise that Bill's crucifixion possibly signals for Bertha a deliverance from sentimentality that may presage her ability to deal ruthlessly with the type of men who victimize her and the gang throughout the film.

Is there the suggestion here that the audience, too, is to purge itself of traditional ideas concerning the place of violence in social and political evolution if any change in the working man's status in America is to be effected? Perhaps so. Again, the viewer is thrown back to the recurring question that *Boxcar Bertha* raises: is violence perpetrated against the violent, and performed in the name of a just cause (as Von's is towards the film's end), justifiable? Certainly, during the highly emotional moments depicting Bill's crucifixion[7] and its aftermath (we must remember that although he has escaped from jail and is strictly speaking a fugitive, Bill is at this point rather old and feeble), the audience is virtually forced to demand vengeance for the act's cruelty. We want to see justice done, and it is done: Von murders all of the thugs, with Scorsese sparing us none of the details of their murders.

How this moral question is to be resolved is left open at the film's end. Throughout *Boxcar Bertha*, the railroad line has acted as a symbol of both life (Bertha and Bill's tender, affectionate moments in boxcars) and death (present in the Reader Corporation's ruthlessness and exemplified by the many injuries and deaths perpetrated on or near railroad lines). At the film's end, though, the railroad ironically becomes a catalyst of transcendence. Having literally and figuratively "lived by" the railroad, Bill now dies by it as well—at the hands of Sartoris's thugs, who beat him and then nail him to a boxcar.

Although Bill's absence will be perceived as a grievous loss by Bertha, his sacrifice may, like that of Jesus, be an inspiration to others, who will perhaps be encouraged to emulate Bill's best qualities: his dedication, fervency, and life-oriented belief in the cause of the disadvantaged. Moreover, Bill's crucifixion quite possibly creates a martyr for the labor movement. For the majority of *Boxcar Bertha*'s last shots, Scorsese positions the camera behind the door of the car to which Bill has been nailed, so that all one sees are the four outstretched fingers of Bill's left hand and, below on the ground, Bertha staring up at him. As the train begins to pull away, Bertha follows Bill and then loses him (all the while screaming "Don't take him, don't take him," as though he is not only being delivered away from her and unto his people but is also somehow being elevated to some form of lasting enshrinement, as in "the angels took him up"). Bill's fingers point screen left, possibly suggesting that the leftist orientation of the labor movement should continue until a proper balance between the right-wing factionalism of the country's Sartorises and the revolutionary demands of the working class is achieved. Although we cannot see Bertha in the film's last few seconds, it is visually implied that instead of merely disappearing she is somehow, like Bill, on the brink of apotheosis herself, since she is not only lost to view near the frame's top, but becomes virtually invisible as the film stock's graininess can no longer adequately resolve her diminishing figure, which in a populist fashion seems to blend in with the surrounding countryside. The manner of presentation of Bill's death and Bertha's figurative "disappearance" signal eventual symbolic ascension for them both, thus leaving us with a powerful feeling of future possibilities that brands the film as one of hope, not despair, and its message as one of renewal, not destruction.

NOTES

1.   One might almost view the characters of Sartoris and Bill as a father and son pair, the elder bitterly passed beyond his youth's idealism into a pessimistic maturity in which only money matters. Bill, though, quite possibly represents Sartoris as a young man, rich with ideas and desires.

2.   The animal stupidity of Sartoris's two main killers is aptly demonstrated when, after Bertha—who is holding a gun on them—tells the men to first "sit down," then "stand up," then "sit down;" the film moves on to the next scene in which Sartoris, as though he were talking to a pair of trained dogs, tells the men to "sit . . . sit down."

3.   For a film with such a hellfire and damnation attitude about the polarization of rich versus poor, it is surprising that *Boxcar Bertha* contains only one biblical reference, which occurs during an

exchange between Bill and Sartoris. Still, this exchange is
sufficiently strong to characterize the two men.

During a robbery, as Bill is gathering Sartoris's dinner
guests' valuables, which he places in a silver vase (Sartoris, with
characteristic upper-class disdain, says, "You probably think [that] is
a cuspidor"), Sartoris remarks, "Lay not up treasure on the earth,"
an ironic comment given his own wealth. Bill essays to finish the
reference for him: ". . . where thieves break through and steal."
However, as Sartoris points out, Bill's quote is not only incomplete
but incorrect, since it omits the reference to the deadly, corrupting,
natural erosions of wealth ("moths and rust") and the injunction to
instead "lay up treasures in heaven." This latter rejoinder is a part
of the quote Bill would characteristically be expected to forget, since
it encourages ignoring one's poverty on earth in favor of some "pie
in the sky" reward in the afterlife. Through the omissions, then, Bill
indicates that he relies, not on salvation in another, supposedly better
world, but on some form of deliverance through direct action in this
one.

Thus, referring to his gun during this sequence, Bill tells
Sartoris, "This here's my Bible," thereby giving voice to a sentiment
whose justification seems hard to avoid, since we have already seen
how necessary the use of guns to counter the forces of the rich seems
to be (as when Bertha saves Rake from harm by shooting a fat
gambler). However, further consideration indicates that the use of
firearms in the film can also be condemned. In the gambling
sequence, Rake was, after all, cheating, and therefore deserved to be
caught; while the use of guns by the gang can simultaneously be
viewed as a proper response to the excesses of Sartoris and his thugs,
as well as a deplorable fall from grace.

4. When Bill is in jail, Bertha turns to prostitution for money. In one
scene, intending to take a client to her room, Bertha accidentally
opens the door to another room in which Scorsese and Gayne
Rescher are occupied with a nude woman. The woman is standing
up, with her back to Rescher; Scorsese, sitting on the bed, faces her
front. When Bertha opens the door, Scorsese says in a friendly way,
"Come on in." One can only guess what the two "clients" are doing,
although the director's invitation to join in anticipates his appearance
in the back of Travis's cab in *Taxi Driver*, during which he has the
helpless Travis participate in his spying on a woman whom the
character played by Scorsese refers to as his "wife."

5. The music in the film complements and, to a certain extent,
determines our emotional reactions to the scenes in which it is
employed. Harmonica music is used for its evocative effect. This
type of accompaniment first appears during the film's opening

sequence, in which Bertha and Von watch Bertha's father piloting his
plane. The music reappears when Bertha has taken up residence in
Mrs. Mailer's whorehouse and is doubtless recalling the days when,
in stark contrast to her present situation, she was still innocent (a
quality communicated when, in the first scene, she absentmindedly
lifts her skirt to scratch her thigh, a gesture that Bill, working on a
nearby railroad gang, is quick to appreciate; the contrast between
Bertha's sexual naivete and Bill's experience appears once again
when they take refuge in a boxcar after the riot). Indeed, it is the
sound of harmonica music coming from a cafe that causes Bertha in
a later scene (by which point she is already an experienced prostitute)
to look in and discover Von, with whom she is touchingly reunited.

Bluegrass music is the film's predominant accompaniment,
used to complement the enthusiastic, idealistic feelings of ecstasy and
freedom engendered during the gang's daring robberies and
getaways. The music first appears in modified form as simple fiddle
music during the fight involving Bill, the man who hired Mr.
Thompson, the man's black chauffeur, and Von. With its conflict
between rich and poor, the scene contains in seminal form the germ
of the gang's later revolt. As a consequence, when the gang begin
methodically robbing the railroad, the bluegrass music reappears; this
time, though, in keeping with the gang's self-conscious behavior, the
music is more developed. It is now played by a fiddle, banjo, and
harmonica, the last instrument introducing a slight evocative effect
that recalls the gang's innocent days before they became thieves.

6.   This sequence between Bertha and Bill ends with the sound of a
gunshot (either Von or Rake has fired his gun) which, through
juxtaposition of sound and image, links the personal and public lives
that the lovers unsuccessfully attempt to keep separate; the moral
compromise involved with the gang's turning to crime inevitably
infects their private relationships. The unsuccessful separation of the
two spheres has been implied earlier in the film during the sequence
in which Rake, presumably safe in a boxcar, lights his cigar at the
same time as Sartoris's thugs are setting fire to a camp inhabited by
a number of itinerants, Bill among them.

7.   Bill's comparison to Jesus (and, thereby, Jesus' eventual crucifixion)
is anticipated earlier when Bill, alone among the gang members (all
of whom have taken refuge in a church named "Nazarene"), is seen
standing where the church's altar would have been located and posing
in front of a mural depicting Jesus.

Chapter Three

THE NEIGHBORHOOD

Viewers familiar with *Who's That Knocking at My Door* will realize from *Mean Streets'* first few minutes that the latter film is in many ways a continuation of the earlier work's thematic concerns. What they may not be prepared for, though, is the striking manner in which Scorsese has developed his directorial skills in the intervening six years, enabling him to produce a film whose structural integrity and emotional impact is greater than anything he has ever done before.

Mean Streets begins with a disturbing dream (experienced by Harvey Keitel's Charlie) and ends with an outburst of violence that easily qualifies as a nightmare. Yet even Charlie's dream has something of a nightmarish anxiety about it. Instead of opening with titles, the film begins in total blackness—the blackness of Charlie's sleep, a realm empty of everything but words. "You don't make up for your sins in church; you do it in the street, you do it at home. The rest is bullshit and you know it." After this internalized pronouncement, Charlie wakes up.

In the conflict between the desire for church-sanctioned and church-dispensed absolution and the kind of redemption (if indeed one is available) that may be obtained in the streets, Charlie's statement demonstrates that its speaker is clearly the philosophical heir to *Knocking*'s J.R. The difference, though, is that where in *Knocking* J.R. exemplified the antagonism between the secular and religious spheres (resorting to the latter to compensate for his shortcomings in the former), no voice in the film was given to the inevitable conflict that such a bifurcated view of reality entails. In *Mean Streets*, this conflict is expressly acknowledged in Charlie's statement, although the film shows us that this problem has not been resolved. The self-assured voice that offers the above statement is not that of the Charlie who acts in the film but that of his inner self, the conscience that gnaws at him throughout *Mean Streets* as he attempts to resolve the

25

contradictions between the things that he does (missing appointments with his uncle; trying to break up with his girlfriend, Teresa; acting as a protective cover for his friend Johnny Boy; making a date with the black dancer, Diane) and the things that he inwardly knows he should do (be punctual; pay attention to his uncle; try to stand by Teresa; realize that Johnny Boy is just using him; stay away from Diane).[1]

One of the shocking things about *Mean Streets* is that the crude justice meted out at the film's end seems somehow deserved, this in spite of the fact that we also hope Charlie will continue to do the precise things that precipitate the attack: protect Johnny Boy and, at the same time, remain true to Teresa. Yet to hope that Charlie would somehow act differently is to believe in the possibility of alternative modes of behavior. Instead, *Mean Streets* makes clear that the characters are trapped by their milieu's claustrophobic atmosphere. If *Mean Streets*' characters are to survive, they must act in definite ways; there simply are no choices if one is to prosper. One must conform to the Italian community's prevailing (even if objectionable) values or court disaster. The film's streets are mean because they are all dead ends.[2]

Waking from the anxious dream, Charlie gets out of bed and passes a cross on the wall, omnipresent sign of the church's influence and ironic symbol of the kind of selfless sacrifice which the surviving characters in the film realize is impossible if one is to endure. As in *Knocking*, Scorsese then employs the film's soundtrack to communicate and suggest themes and meanings. Here, as Charlie traverses the room, traffic sounds and police sirens can be heard invading the relative calm, blunt reminders of the noisy, hazardous street life of which Charlie is, as we are to see, such an integral part.

Scorsese then cuts to a shot of an eight-millimeter projector; as it whirs, we are shown the film it is projecting (as in *Alice*'s opening, the included film is framed smaller than the full size of the 35mm frame, thus making us doubly aware of both the 8mm movie within a 35mm movie and alternatively, the movie within which the smaller-sized movie takes place). In essence, the effect of the home movie's inclusion is to remind us that the entirety of what we are watching is a crafted representation, an artifact that demands attention to the manner in which it is constructed if we are to appreciate its significance.

The home movie begins with a piece of leader; a viewer who closely examines a film print or video of *Mean Streets* can divine the writing that appears on this short strip of film. Although some of the written words are obscured by thick black divisions between the frames, enough of the writing can be read to determine that the leader labels the following home movie (and by extension the entirety of the feature film that follows) as the "Scorsese baptism." Literally, of course, these words refer to the baby whose baptism is celebrated in part of the home movie footage, but the words may apply as well to the baptism into the doctrines of growing up Italian in New York's Little Italy that is visited upon three different groups: the characters in *Mean Streets* who have already been successfully baptized into the manner of prospering in Little Italy (Michael and Tony); those who, while literally baptized, must go through another baptism (this time a blood baptism) if they are truly to appreciate the community's moral code (Charlie, Johnny Boy, and Teresa); and finally, the audience itself which, exposed to the film's events, is baptized into knowledge of the assumptions and beliefs that underlie the Italian-American experience.

I have already noted some of these assumptions in the discussion of *Who's That Knocking at My Door*. In *Mean Streets*, the consequences of unsuccessfully resolving antithetical desires are much more harmful than in the earlier film. It is no longer a question, as it was for J.R., of merely deciding whether one prefers the company of one's male friends over the love and companionship of a woman (the fact that such a polarized, absurd choice is even seriously considered is itself evidence of J.R.'s unnatural situation). Instead, the price paid in *Mean Streets* for failing properly to balance the values and demands of the community with one's personal desires is either banishment from the community (as happens with the young assassin from Tony's bar) or near-lethal injury (the fate visited on Charlie, Johnny Boy, and Teresa). In effect, *Mean Streets* significantly raises *Knocking*'s stakes from personal and romantic set-back to life-threatening cataclysm. The earlier film's death of emotion here becomes the possible literal death of one's self.

After the home movie ends, the main action of *Mean Streets* begins. First we see Little Italy's annual San Gennaro feast. Immediately after this establishing shot, Scorsese cuts to a shot inside the bathroom of Tony's bar, the first of four such sequences that are used to introduce the film's central male characters. Tony (David Proval) discovers a junkie in the bathroom and throws him out of the bar. Scorsese then superimposes the name "Tony" as a subtitle.

This attempt to clean things up is clearly a characteristic pose for Tony. Yet, as we see from *Mean Streets'* ensuing action, his efforts are in vain. The bar is host to fights, drunkenness, disagreements, even a murder. There is no conceivable way that Tony can keep the pollution of the neighborhood street life from infecting his place of business. Like the young man sticking the needle into his arm, Tony and his friends are addicts, not to drugs but to an equally potent force: their corrupt milieu, which creates a dependency so powerful that it can never be broken.

Next seen is Michael (Richard Romanus), the neighborhood hustler, who loans money and deals in stolen goods—camera accessories, cigarettes, even toilet paper that has been stolen from an army PX. Michael attempts to sell what he claims are "German lenses, the best kind . . . telescopic." As the man to whom he is speaking tells him, though, all he has taken receipt of are "adapters . . . Jap adapters." The foul-up is cruelly comic; Michael adopts a pained look and stares off into space, while Scorsese flashes his name on the screen. The situation aptly sums up Michael as a cheap, ignorant man who, judging from his vignette, will never amount to very much. Michael is a young man destined to be taken advantage of in stupid deals (even the kids from Riverdale who are looking for fireworks short-change him), a characteristic which prepares us for the way that Johnny Boy continually fails to make his loan payments to him. Until *Mean Streets'* end (when, through violence, he legitimizes his claim to being serious about collecting the money owed to him), Michael is seen as incapable of adeptly handling his business affairs.

The following sequence introduces us to Johnny Boy (Robert De Niro), the aberrant whose disregard for prescribed behavior labels him as Charlie's opposite. Where Charlie is always officious and polite, trying whenever possible to placate offended parties, always playing by the rules, exercising verbal and physical restraint to accomplish his ends (characteristics for which Johnny criticizes him, as we learn later in the film when Johnny says of Charlie, "Charlie likes everybody, everybody likes Charlie, a fucking politician"), Johnny Boy is imprudent in both word and deed. He will not keep quiet when the billiard parlor owner, fat Joey, offers payment on a bet; even after the pool hall fight, Johnny risks another violent confrontation by calling Joey a "scum bag." For Johnny, frankness is preferable to seeing people get the money that they deserve.

Johnny is also given to random, pointless acts of violence, another activity frowned upon in the neighborhood. As Charlie's mafioso uncle, Giovanni (Cesare Danova), makes clear, violence is a tool to be used only when necessary, and then in the proper way. One does not pressure or threaten a restaurant owner if he cannot meet his loan payment; one shows restraint.[3] One does not shoot a man merely to avenge someone else's honor (as the assassin does in Tony's bar). Such techniques are not practical in the contemporary world; a low profile must be maintained. As the prevailing voice of the community, Giovanni would doubtless condemn Johnny's wanton acts of destruction (such as his firing a pistol off a roof one night in a playful attempt to shatter the light on the top of the Empire State Building). Thus, Johnny Boy's characteristic act in his vignette introduction is to blow up a mailbox and then run away. This foolhardy deed followed by flight defines for us the behavior that he exhibits throughout the film (in which he is often seen fleeing across rooftops and down fire escapes, running at various times through the streets) until, at *Mean Streets'* end, his recklessness catches up with him.

The sirens heard after the mailbox explosion carry over into the next scene, which finds Charlie in church; the identity of sound establishes a simultaneity of time. Characteristically, while Johnny Boy is causing trouble, Charlie is looking for a redemptive, penitential way out of dilemmas. The casually dressed and coiffed Johnny Boy views excessive actions as expressions of his freedom; Charlie—the more repressed of the two (as evidenced by his impeccable dress and conservative haircut)—goes to church seeking a release from his anxieties.

He does not find it, though. Unlike *Knocking*'s J.R., Charlie clearly realizes the contradictions between a redemption limited in scope and application (it does not speak to situations involving physical desire and cannot be applied to the problems one encounters in street life) and the kind of saving grace that may be derived from the support of one's friends. Charlie knows that his life and the lives of his friends are not blameless; he acknowledges the need for some form of restitution. But he also realizes that the church cannot make such restitution available to him. As he says of the confessional and the penance that the priest routinely doles out to him, "Those things (the Hail Marys and Our Fathers) don't mean anything to me; they're just words." It is at the end of this church sequence that Charlie's name is flashed onto the screen. Only Charlie has been afforded two characterizing vignettes, one at the film's beginning, one here at the end of its introductory section. His two vignettes bracket the others (as the bread-breaking sequence brackets the straitened universe of *Who's That Knocking at My Door*), enclosing the characters in a structure whose form reflects the limitations of the strongly proscribed lives that they lead.

Charlie's realization that salvation cannot be attained in church is purely intellectual, though, not spiritual. Charlie knows that the church can offer him nothing, yet he returns there nonetheless—either literally (as when we see him kneeling in prayer before the altar) or allusively, as in the repeated references associated with him to blessings. (For example, before the pool hall fight, fat Joey, calling Charlie "Saint Charles," asks him to "bless my balls," a mocking, playful statement which reaffirms the film's seriously posited relation between religion and sexuality and the conflict, especially in Charlie, between the two realms.)

Charlie may attempt to make a joke out of his spiritual obsession, may try to minimize the part that his inner voice plays in his life, but he cannot. His concern with damnation clearly indicates this. Damnation—present in his discussion about the two kinds of Hell-fire ("the kind you can feel with your hand . . . the kind you can feel with your soul")—is one of his constant concerns. Throughout the film—at the bar, at a table, in the kitchen of Oscar's restaurant—Charlie is seen thrusting his fingers into fire. This literal playing with purgation symbolizes both Charlie's reckless and foolhardy "playing with fire" by continuing to associate with Johnny Boy (as Giovanni tells Charlie, "Watch yourself; don't spoil anything; honorable men go with honorable men") and Teresa, as well as his anticipation of the painful Hell-fires (comically represented by a scene he watches from Roger Corman's *The Tomb of Ligeia*) that he expects await him in the afterlife.

Charlie clearly expresses this fixation on damnation: "If I do something wrong I want to pay for it my way, so I do my own penance for my own sins, and it's all bullshit except the pain, the pain of Hell." This is a convenient philosophy, since it means that Charlie does not necessarily have to do any penance in this life. Charlie goes on to talk about the two kinds of Hell-fire pain, "the physical" and the worst kind, "the spiritual." On this last word, Scorsese cuts to a slow motion tracking shot inside Tony's bar, suggesting that it is there in this secular church, where much of *Mean Streets*' action takes place, and which is bathed throughout the film in a Hellish red light (red like fire, red like the body's insides)[4], that a significant amount of Charlie's earthly torment occurs.

As Charlie states, though, the worst agony is "the spiritual"; on the final word, Scorsese cuts to a shot of Diane, the bar's dancer with whom Charlie is fascinated (perhaps predominantly because, being black and therefore unacceptable in his uncle's eyes, she is as forbidden as Johnny Boy and Teresa). It is ironic that we see Diane as Charlie pronounces the word "spiritual," since her appeal for Charlie is purely physical (as he puts it, "She's really good looking, really good looking"). The sequence's juxtaposition of the spiritual and physical suggests that the confusion about what to do, to which we are here being exposed, is in Charlie's mind (as he observes at the above statement's end, "But she's black"). Indeed, throughout the film, Charlie behaves as though he is two different people: one who knows how he should act, and one who feels he should do just the opposite. Ultimately, though, Charlie is weak. Unlike Johnny Boy, Teresa, Michael, and Tony, Charlie does not really know what he wants; throughout *Mean Streets* he stands at the crossroads of intellectual resolve and physical and emotional desire without being able to decide what to do. He is in turn sympathetic with Michael, then sympathetic with Michael's adversary, Johnny; he rejects Teresa on his Uncle's advice, then regrets the decision.

If Johnny Boy represents Charlie's impulsive side, the part of him that goes ahead and makes a date with Diane, then Giovanni represents the cold, judgmental part of Charlie's personality, the part that Charlie thinks should not predominate because it is in conflict with his major emotional priorities: his attachment to Johnny Boy and Teresa (although it is unclear whether Charlie would really be concerned about Johnny Boy were he not involved with Teresa, who is Johnny's cousin. Of course, the reverse may also be true).

For Giovanni, Teresa is not an epileptic; she is "sick in the head." We may infer that he feels the same way about Johnny who is, ironically, named after him. Similarly, commenting on restaurant owner Oscar's partner, Groppi, who one evening puts a gun in his mouth and pulls the trigger (the bullet's discharge is depicted in a completely white flash frame; *Mean Streets* gives us virtually no blood until its final cataclysm), Giovanni comments, "That Groppi was always half crazy, half crazy to say the least." For Giovanni, then, any individual who exhibits behavior different from the norm (Johnny's recklessness; Teresa's desire—which Giovanni views as consistent with her physical aberration—that, contrary to her parents' wishes, she have her own apartment; Groppi's disappearance and suicide) is "sick in the head." One either behaves according to Giovanni's expectations or one is summarily dismissed as an aberrant.

Charlie is continually provided with examples of the recklessness of his decision to remain sympathetic with Johnny and Teresa. Thus, the first time that Johnny appears in the film after the opening vignettes, he walks into Tony's bar without any pants on. Charlie realizes how absurd Johnny's entrance makes him, his protector, look, and recognizes how ridiculous it is to continue his allegiance to his friend. Yet his internal monologue during Johnny's slow-motion entrance suggests that he views Johnny's behavior as a form of humiliation that he must bear in order to improve himself. "Thanks a lot, Lord, we talk about penance and this walks through the door; well, we play by your rules, don't we?" he says, thereby speaking to God in the bar, the church of the streets, just as directly as he addressed religious questions to himself while he was in the actual church earlier. In this secular church, though, one does not aspire to and desire Paradise; here, one ruminates on the notion of Hell.

Charlie apparently sees Johnny as the cross he must bear as a necessary prelude to his redemption. Teresa, too, becomes for Charlie not only a source of pleasure (like her cousin, with whom Charlie kids around at various points) but pain as well, as in his anxious arguments with her. Just as Charlie sacrifices some of his credibility for Johnny's sake (he pledges to Michael that Johnny will make his loan payment, although Johnny doesn't), so too is Charlie seen in a sacrificial position with Teresa (as when, making love to her, he stretches out both of his arms, adopting the posture of someone being crucified), a sacrificial aspect later reflected in the cross-shaped *fleur de lys* patterns of the wallpaper outside a hotel room in which he and Teresa have a liaison.

However, neither Johnny nor Teresa is a totally sympathetic character. Johnny takes advantage of Charlie's intercessions on his behalf, while Teresa is at times portrayed as extremely rude. This aspect is apparent when she tells Michael to "fuck off," and especially when she is cruel to the cleaning woman in the hall outside the hotel room where she and Charlie meet. Johnny and Teresa's nastiness not only adds depth to their characters but relieves us of the burden of believing that Charlie is martyring himself for the sake of supposedly admirable people.

Scorsese employs a number of techniques in *Mean Streets* to both embody and prefigure the film's actions and meanings. As in *Who's That Knocking at My Door*, music plays an important role. *Mean Streets* opens with "Be My Baby," a song that accompanies the baptismal film. We may infer from this juxtaposition of song and image that the "baby" referred to is as much the child being baptized as the entire community and its values, values affirmed for the participants and observers in the baptismal ceremony. In this sense, "Be My Baby" is a request, not for emotional fulfillment but—given the film's claustrophobic setting—for spiritual and moral entrapment.

When Charlie enters Tony's bar towards the film's beginning, The Rolling Stones' "Tell Me" is employed. The lyric "Tell me you're coming back to me" takes on the suggested meaning of a return to a loved one (in this case, the bar, which represents the neighborhood that Charlie loves), a tragic desire when we consider that the precise manner in which Charlie takes the neighborhood to heart initiates the downward spiral of events which culminates in the film's final blowout.

Johnny Boy's entrance is appropriately accompanied by "Jumping Jack Flash." The song not only mirrors Johnny's neighborhood nickname (at one point, Michael asks, "Where's Flash?") but also suggests explosions, a number of which (the blown-up mailbox, the gunfire off the roof, the homemade bomb that he tosses, as well as the flashes from Michael's hired killer's gun) Johnny occasions. The word "flash" may also be taken as referring to a transitory spark of brightness, an apt metaphor for the behavior of this emotionally volatile, fast-talking character. And, as we might expect, the song sums up Johnny's entire attitude about his reckless actions; rather than regretting them we see that, in the song's words, he thinks them "a gas."

When Charlie makes his date with Diane,[5] "Please Come Back To Me" plays on the soundtrack as an ironic anticipation of Charlie's failure to return from his day's rounds to keep his appointment. Preparing for a party, Charlie's affection for the neighborhood is affirmed in "I Love You So." At the party, Charlie is dancing with a drunk young woman and at the precise moment that she passes out in his arms, the background music trumpets forth the comical lyric, "I'll never part from you and your loving ways."

Finally, towards *Mean Streets'* conclusion, Scorsese once again uses music as an ironic counterpoint to the film's action. When Charlie and Johnny are about to leave the city in Tony's car, "Mickey's

Monkey" plays on the soundtrack. The song's title acts as an accurate indication of Johnny Boy's present condition. Having just humiliated Michael in the bar, Johnny apparently thinks that he has "made a monkey" out of the loan shark. In truth, the opposite is the case. Johnny is the monkey who belongs to Michael (Mickey). At this point, Johnny is nothing more than a skittish beast at the end of a chain whose slack Michael will soon pull in.

Traditional music is employed to complement characters and settings viewed as more conventional (and well-adjusted) than those belonging to the film's rock-saturated youth milieu. Giovanni's musical accompaniment is either opera or old-style Italian songs. Both types of music are sung in Italian, the language that Giovanni, as the representative of the status quo, usually speaks when he is talking business (even when in conversation with his uncle, though, Charlie slips back into using English). One can see Charlie and Giovanni, then, as representing the new and the old ways of life. One of the tragedies that *Mean Streets* depicts is that the old ways are, apparently, the only ways. It is only the traditionally-oriented characters—those like Giovanni and Michael—who survive and prosper. In a petty way, Michael mirrors Giovanni's financial concerns; his entrance into the bar towards *Mean Streets'* end to collect his money in old-style fashion is appropriately accompanied by an Italian language song, a type of song whose association with revenge was presaged when it played during Johnny's immediately preceding flight, and which continues on into part of the assassination sequence. Tony also may be considered a survivor, a young man who has somehow learned to prosper, to live successfully with the perennial, oppressive beast of the past (thus his ability to safely enter the cage with his pet lion cub while all that his friends can do is cower in the corners of the room).[6]

The conclusion to be drawn from this schema is clear: there is no real future for the next generation in Little Italy, only the promise of the past's repetition. The film's characters must conform to the old ways. One does not flaunt tradition. One pays the loan shark, even if it is only a token amount (but not the insultingly meager ten dollars that Johnny Boy offers Michael). One does not, as Teresa tries to, disobey one's parents. And one stays, as Charlie should have, only "with honorable men."

True, Charlie's emotional loyalty to Johnny and Teresa is admirable, but as *Mean Streets* demonstrates, the death of such emotions is necessary if one is to survive. One must be cold like

Giovanni (as Giovanni characteristically says to Charlie about Teresa, "You live next door; keep an eye opened but don't get involved") or cold like Giovanni's counterpart, Michael (even when splattered with cake and icing at the party, Michael sits quietly, cool and detached). To be lukewarm like the wavering Charlie, or volatile like Johnny Boy, is simply not smart. Unfortunately, Charlie is unable to achieve such emotional distance from events.[7]

While *Mean Streets* exhibits an impressive sense of energy, the film's arena of action is strikingly restrained. Predominantly, the action is not only limited to the neighborhood but takes place for the most part in dark rooms, cramped corners, and cluttered, smoky bars. This sense of enclosure carries over to the type of camera work that Scorsese employs, which rarely opens up the action. Instead, complementing and increasing the already created sense of containment, the camera is pushed right up against the characters, accentuating their facial characteristics (pores, sweat, anxious expressions) and also thereby giving the audience very little breathing room between themselves and what they are watching.

This is not to suggest that *Mean Streets*' camera is always stationary. One immediately thinks of the numerous handheld tracking shots in the film, from Johnny's slow-motion barroom entrance to the photography during the poolroom fight, during which the hand-held camera follows the action around the room.

In the midst of the party at Tony's bar, the camera, in slow-motion mode, is slaved to a dolly; riding along on the dolly with the camera, Charlie is thereby maintained at a constant distance from it as it loops its way through the bar. Although the effect of the antagonism between Charlie's rigidly stationary position and the careening background is vertiginous (thus expressing his drunken state), no sense of freedom is created. Instead, Charlie's physical enslavement to the camera's point of view reaffirms the feeling of entrapment that the film has already occasioned.

The sense of entrapment that characterizes *Mean Streets* is complemented by the number of fateful foreshadowings that the film employs as reminders that the future of all the characters is already written. Before Robert Carradine (the assassin) enters Tony's bathroom, where he intends to murder a drunk (played by his brother David) who (we later learn) has insulted a local resident, Charlie asks Carradine if he'd like to play "a little blackjack." The game of chance and the deadly color black provide a rude announcement of the action that is to follow. Later, after Tony and Michael have conned a couple of suburbanite kids out of some money, they pick up Charlie and go to the movies. The scene from *The Searchers* that we see them watching shows us the fight between two friends (Martin Pawley and Charlie McCorry) over a woman, an action that prefigures the fight between two other cinematic friends,[8] Charlie and Johnny, which occurs partially as a result of their disagreement over the extent of Charlie's involvement with Teresa.

But perhaps the most frightening anticipations are those that prefigure the shooting of Charlie and Johnny at the film's end. A glimpse of a wheel of chance at the San Gennaro feast (a festival celebrating the bloody martyrdom of Saint Januarius, Sicily's patron saint) reminds us of how, having virtually repudiated the certainty of his future with Giovanni, Charlie is now a victim of fate. Later, as he stands outside the movie theater where he saw *The Tomb of Ligeia*, Charlie is bordered by posters for two significant films: *X: The Man with the X-Ray Eyes* (whose protagonist's tragically acute vision contrasts with Charlie's self-imposed blindness) and *Point Blank*, a film about a shadow world of threat and aggression where, as in *Mean Streets*, no perceptible enemy may be identified and isolated. Significantly, the gun held by Lee Marvin in the *Point Blank* poster points towards Charlie, just as the gun wielded by Michael's assassin will soon be directed at him, Johnny, and Teresa.

Repeatedly throughout *Mean Streets*, Charlie and Johnny draw attention to their hands and their necks, the two parts of the body (Charlie in the hand, Johnny in the neck) in which they are shot;[9] these innocent gestures thus take on fateful overtones. When he has Johnny stay over with him, Charlie at one point gets out of bed and rubs the side of his neck. Later, when he is talking to Giovanni in a restaurant, he scratches the side of his neck, as though somehow anticipating the precise location where his friend will be shot.

After the barroom assassination sequence, Charlie and Johnny enter a graveyard and sit on the tombstones. The scene's morbidity is complemented by the sound of a woman's scream which comes from a nearby party, a sound that anticipates Teresa's scream in the car after Charlie and Johnny have been shot. Later, walking along with Charlie after leaving the graveyard, Johnny stops to admire a small gun (possibly similar to the one Michael's assassin will use) in a store window and, as he does so, brings his hands up to his neck to adjust his collar.

Significantly, three more instances of this type of gesture occur. In the bar after Michael has arrived for the pay-off, Johnny calls Michael "a fucking jerk-off," at which point Tony rubs his neck, unconsciously anticipating (as Charlie has done) Johnny's fate. Charlie and Johnny then get into an argument about Johnny's behavior, after which Charlie once again touches his neck. Even after the argument ends and Charlie and Johnny have left the bar, the foreshadowings continue. This time, after Johnny's manic outburst, Charlie hits his friend in the neck to sober him up, an effect that Johnny's being shot in the same place will undoubtedly have on him.

Perhaps the most shocking presentiment of danger, though, occurs while Giovanni discusses with two of the assassin's relatives the shooting of the drunk in Tony's bar. At a decisive point in their talk, Giovanni states that the young assassin will have to leave New York for a while. Then, in a dictatorial pronouncement delivered in the kind of decisive, cold voice that one could easily imagine Giovanni using to pronounce a death sentence, Giovanni says, "Get rid of him." On these words, Scorsese cuts to a tight shot of Giovanni's right hand. Giovanni's omnipresent small cigar is thrust between his fingers; his hand passes horizontally over the table's upright sugar dispenser. The conjunction of the deadly pronouncement with the upright dispenser and the phallic cigar establishes a linkage between death and potency that appears three other times in the film.

When the drunk is shot in the bathroom, he is leaning against the wall, holding his penis in his hand. Just before he fires, the assassin unfurls his long black hair: the deadly confrontation thus takes on a sexual suggestiveness. In another scene, Charlie and Teresa, the film's major heterosexual couple, are in bed together:[10] at one point, Charlie makes believe his hand is a gun and shoots her while on the soundtrack a gunshot is heard. This deadly game between lovers not only anticipates the later shooting of Charlie, Johnny, and Teresa[11]; its juxtaposition of morbidity (the pretend gun) and sexuality (the intimate setting, the phallic finger-as-gun-barrel) reappears in Charlie's dream about Teresa, whose most powerful image is Charlie's penis coming blood: the organ of reproductive life here connotes death. Finally, after Johnny has taunted Michael in Tony's bar by refusing to pay him enough, Johnny offers two gestures: a threat with an empty gun (in contrast to the loaded gun that Michael will soon have his hired killer use) and, as Michael is leaving, a dry-hump motion to communicate to Michael that in screwing him out of the money Johnny has, in effect, fucked him up the ass. In each case, the traditional symbols of male potency (the cigar, the hand-as-gun, the penis in the dream, Johnny's gun and penis gestures) accompany a gesture and/or a piece of dialogue that, instead of connoting productive life, suggests sterility, finality, figurative death. Apparently, traditional symbols of potency in the film's universe have failed; they have been replaced by symbols of death and impotence. Even Giovanni's power and resolve are implicitly criticized; in contrast to Charlie, Giovanni's coolness makes him appear like a corpse.

In reprising the film's opening vignette technique, *Mean Streets'* finale returns us to the film's beginning, as though we have been stuck in the same place for almost two hours (an effect that complements the film's static atmosphere). After the shooting of Charlie, Teresa, and Johnny Boy, we see Tony washing his hands. Charlie, too (like his friend Tony), had wanted to stay clear of the neighborhood's taint by being uninvolved (thus Charlie's symbolic washing of his hands while Giovanni consigned the young assassin to oblivion) but he had failed. Tony had suggested to Charlie that he repudiate his pointless religious view, the one that involves compassion, but Charlie did not take his advice. "Why do you let those guys [the priests, with their patently absurd stories about redemption and retribution] get to you?" he asks Charlie. "You gotta be like me if you're gonna be safe." Even though locked in the neighborhood, Tony has learned how to tame the beast of his surroundings, but Charlie cannot emulate his friend.

We next see Giovanni watching a television film which depicts a young woman being lifted supine out of a wrecked car, an image that shockingly matches our view of Teresa being helped out of Charlie's crashed car after the shooting. Characteristically, Giovanni retains his composure in the face of this violent image. Diane is seen coolly lighting a cigarette. Nothing has changed for her; she sits alone. As she probably expected it would, Charlie's promise of a hostess job in his pipe-dream club has come to naught; consequently, she wears the same ironic expression that she displayed when Charlie first mentioned the idea to her. Michael and his gunman recline peacefully in their car; having carried out their homicidal mission and wreaked the revenge that the law of the community dictates, they can sit and relax.

As for Johnny Boy and Charlie, Johnny is seen, no longer running jauntily as usual, but stumbling along the street, holding his neck as he weaves down a fire lane; Charlie, sunk penitentially onto his

knees outside the wrecked car, stares ahead blankly, uncompre-
hendingly, as a police siren (reprising a sound from *Mean Streets'*
beginning) is heard in the distance, after which a patrol car pulls up.

Scorsese ends the film with two symbols of tragic closure. He
takes us back to the San Gennaro feast and gives us a bitterly apt song
from the feast ("There's No Place Like Home"). While a blithe
"Thank you, thank you" from a television show blares on the
soundtrack, followed by a depressingly joyous-sounding "buona notte"
from one of the feast's participants, *Mean Streets* winds down to a
close. The film ends with a street-side shot of a woman in a brightly
lit apartment pulling down a window shade, thus figuratively shutting
out the light of hope and redemption and, in the process, closing the
all-seeing eye of the film on this claustrophobic, death-oriented
neighborhood and the tragically limited individuals who are trapped
within its morbid confines.

NOTES

1.   This inner voice continues to hound Charlie throughout the film. It
is this voice that delivers the pronouncements about the two kinds of
pain in Hell. Addressing itself to Charlie's ego, the voice again
appears while Charlie is appreciatively watching Diane, and
comments, "She's really good looking . . . but she's black, you can
see that," as though attempting to teach Charlie's active side how
wrong he would be to go out with her. Consequently, when Charlie
is on his way to meet Diane, the inner voice asks him, "Hey, are you
crazy?" and Charlie tells the cab driver to drive past their
destination.

Charlie's conscience is aware of the destructive power that
he is tempting by his actions in the film; it identifies the flames in the
restaurant grill into which Charlie thrusts his hand as "fire."
Unfortunately, the presence of this voice, which speaks in
contradiction of everything that Charlie does, brands him as an
unintegrated, doubtful misfit, a condition that appears ludicrous to
self-assured characters such as Johnny Boy and Teresa when, towards
the film's end, Charlie allows the voice external expression for the
only time in the film. When he says, "I think you could safely say
that things haven't gone so well tonight but I'm trying, Lord, I'm
trying," all Johnny and Teresa can do is laugh at him.

2.   *Mean Streets'* title derives from a passage in Raymond Chandler's
essay "The Simple Art of Murder," which appears in *The Simple Art
of Murder* (New York: Ballantine Books, 1972, p. 20). Alluding to

someone we may assume to be his ironic private eye, Philip
Marlowe, Chandler wrote,

> In everything that can be called art there is a
> quality of redemption. It may be pure tragedy,
> if it is high tragedy, and it may be the raucous
> laughter of the strong man. But down these
> mean streets a man must go who is not himself
> mean, who is neither tarnished nor afraid. The
> detective in this kind of story must be such a
> man. He is the hero; he is everything. He must
> be a complete man and a common man and yet
> an unusual man. He must be, to use a rather
> weathered phrase, a man of honor—by instinct,
> by inevitability, without thought of it, and
> certainly without saying it.

Clearly, given *Mean Streets'* concern with redemption, and
Charlie's lack of meanness, Charlie could qualify as such a man.
Yet his continual involvement with his uncle, and his trepidation over
the choices he is compelled to make, unfortunately brand him as both
"tarnished" and "afraid." Charlie desires honor, but not the kind of
honor that Giovanni talks about; he wants an honor that surpasses
individual circumstances, one beyond any judgment, one that is,
thereby, essentially unrealistic and unattainable.

3. As Giovanni puts it, "You can help by waiting; don't be impatient."
Then, Charlie's uncle goes on elliptically to foretell who will gain
control of the restaurant as long as Charlie behaves. "You like
restaurants?" he asks.

4. The bar's color is red, like the carpeting in the corridor outside the
hotel room where Charlie and Teresa meet to make love; it thereby
suggests an internal recess in contrast to the corridor's cream-colored
walls and the lightness of the characters' skin tones. Truly, inside
the bar we are exposed to the inner characteristics of most of the
film's principals. It is therefore no surprise that virtually all of the
film's key events (the murder of the drunk; Charlie's agonizing over
his actions and his attraction to Diane; the drunken welcome home
party; the conflicts between Michael and Johnny and, at one point,
Charlie and Teresa; the scene with Tony and his lion) occur in the
bar.

5. Two shots in the sequence involving Charlie's cab ride on his way to
meet Diane anticipate *Taxi Driver*'s camerawork and milieu. One
shot is comprised of a slow point-of-view pan along the street

where Diane is waiting. The nighttime lighting (both cinematographers, *Mean Streets'* Kent Wakeford and *Taxi Driver's* Michael Chapman, intentionally overexpose these respective shots to give them a nightmare garishness), the gaudily-lit stores, the street people silently drifting along—all reappear in *Taxi Driver's* shot in which Travis, looking out from his cab, scans a comparable scene. Similarly, the shot from the top of Charlie's cab, which includes the street scene as an out-of-focus background, also reappears virtually ver-batim in the later film.

6. In this respect, Charlie is just the opposite of the adaptive Tony; their polarized counterpart status is affirmed in their dress for the party at Tony's bar. Tony wears a white tie against a red collar; Charlie wears a red tie against a white collar.

7. Of course, such coolness has its disadvantages as well. Michael and Giovanni are the least humane of all the film's characters. Indeed, Michael and Giovanni's detachment makes them seem more dead than alive.

8. We have seen the use of a film within a film in *Knocking*, in which references to *Rio Bravo*, *Scaramouche*, *The Man Who Shot Liberty Valance*, and *The Searchers* not only commented on the film's action (as *The Searchers* and other film references do in *Mean Streets*) but also reminded us that the "frame" which contains the references is itself a film and thereby demands careful attention if all of its referential language is to be successfully deciphered.

9. Johnny's neck wound also strongly anticipates the neck wound that Travis receives from the caretaker of Iris's apartment building during *Taxi Driver's* extended "blowout" sequence.

10. During this sequence, Teresa asks Charlie why he never tells her he loves her, to which Charlie replies, "Because you're a cunt." Even though something of a bad jest, the statement contains enough serious meaning to establish a link between Charlie and *Knocking's* J.R., who would consider any sexually experienced woman a "whore."

11. This precise hand-as-gun gesture resurfaces at various points in *Taxi Driver*, where it has a similar figurative and fateful effect.

Chapter Four

SHE'S LEAVING HOME

Alice Doesn't Live Here Anymore (1974) represents Scorsese's attempt to produce what might generally be referred to as a women's film. Alice Hyatt (Ellen Burstyn) is a character who possesses a great deal of the director's sympathy, as is clear from her being placed in situations in which it is people other than herself who seem obsessed, greedy, or vengeful. For all of her foul-mouthed wise-cracking, Alice seems for the majority of the film to be a relatively compliant person (perhaps too compliant, as in her servile attitude towards her husband at the film's beginning). Essentially, she is an innocent in a corrupt world, with only the support of her sarcastic son and an occasional friend to sustain her.

One can see the genesis of *New York, New York*'s period look in *Alice*'s stylized beginning. After the film's opening display of the contemporary Warner Bros. logo (a large W superimposed on a black and red background), the film proper begins, immediately reverting to the old Warner Bros. shield logo. This nostalgic recreation is complemented by the significant amount of masking at the frame's edges, as though to suggest that what we are watching here is a film within a film, a dramatization within the drama.[1] Indeed, given the opening scene's exaggerated, stylized set—which includes a garish red sunset in back of a model house—one can assume that what we are seeing is a representation of Alice's memory of her childhood.

This peek into the past is not all sweetness and light, since when the young Alice responds to Alice Faye's "You'll Never Know" by singing a few lines from the song and then commenting, "I could do better, and if anybody doesn't like it they can blow it out their ass," we can see the seeds of the present-day Alice's defensive vulgarity (a trait mimicked by her son).

The transition to the present is slickly accomplished through an echo chamber repetition of the word "now" from the song lyric, a

42

telescoping of the image into the dim recesses of the past, followed by an abrupt plunge into the present. The inset frame is replaced with a full frame, and the Alice Faye song yields to the loud music of Mott the Hoople.

Unlike the young, aggressive Alice, the present-day Alice is woefully worried if anybody (in this case her husband Donald, played by Billy Green Bush) does not approve of what she does. Alice is solicitously concerned about whether or not Donald likes the dinner she has prepared for him (he wolfs it down without tasting it) and tries, unsuccessfully, to engage him in conversation.

What is intriguing about *Alice*'s present-tense opening scene (which includes her son Tommy at the dinner table) is that what we watch at work does not appear to be a family unit. Although we may infer a link between Alice's comic inventiveness (she herself answers the questions she poses to her sullen husband) and her son's prankishness (he substitutes salt for the sugar), there seems to be no cohesiveness among the three people who are sharing dinner. In fact, in his indifference to both Alice and her son, Mr. Hyatt seems less like a true husband and parent than a cruel stranger.

It is essential to note the distinctive ways in which Alice and Tommy (Alfred Lutter) deal with Donald Hyatt. Tommy's response is one of either selfish unconcern (as when he plays his loud music) or barely concealed hostility (the substitution of the salt for the sugar; he knows his mother does not sweeten her drinks, so the joke is solely on Mr. Hyatt). Despite her husband's coolness towards her, though, Alice is extremely deferential. Her son may try to ignore his father, but Alice is completely dependent on Donald for emotional support. Failing to receive such support, the best she can do is either affect nonchalance (exemplified through her kidding) or, like the film's other women (with the notable exception of Flo), resort to tears to get what she wants.

Thus, when Donald later favors the television over Alice, Alice turns away and begins to cry. The tears bring the desired response: Donald turns towards Alice and begins to caress her. We can assume that no matter how genuine her crying is, Alice also knows through experience that such a technique brings her what she desires. Even the barest degree of preconception brands her as a manipulator.

Similarly, although later in the film Alice is obviously weary and depressed after a fruitless job search, understandably breaking down in front of a bar owner (with the result that he buys her a drink and offers her a job), we can again assume that her crying is employed as a manipulative tool. At this point in her life, it is the only way she knows to get what she wants. (Later, Ben's wife will use the device on Alice with similar results.)

Ostensibly opposed to this type of deplorable female manipulation is the character who embodies an alternate form of female behavior: Flo (Diane Ladd), the waitress in Mel's diner. Flo's language not only easily exceeds the mild scatologies that Alice and Tommy employ, but even surpasses the kind of speech of which the diner's clientele seems capable. However, Flo resembles her new co-worker in that she uses her femininity for personal gain. Alice cries to get what she wants; to increase the size of her tips, Flo unbuttons her blouse an extra button down, a strategy she recommends to Alice.

By the time she goes to work at Mel's, Alice is in limbo. Donald's death has thrust her into the world, which she first confronts using the same tools (crying, and an attitude of compliance, which she exhibits with Harvey Keitel's Ben) that she employed in her marriage. Having realized soon after beginning work at Mel's that such strategies are no longer useful, she is left adrift, without an alternative model of behavior. Certainly, Flo is sympathetic to Alice, and after their initial hostility passes, Alice appreciates her friendship. Yet Flo is really nothing more than a replacement for the female friend whom Alice left behind in her old neighborhood. Moreover, both women are still involved in manipulating men to satisfy their needs.

The question arises whether the new person who enters Alice's life at this point (Kris Kristofferson's David) actually represents a change from the kind of behavior that Alice has formerly exhibited and the kind of men with whom she has been associated. David is clearly the third member of the dialectical progress in male relationships that the film shows us (Donald and Ben are the first two parts of the equation). But does he represent (for Alice and for us) a change which would indicate that in some significant way Alice has improved?

The answer to this question is crucial, because on it depends our reading of the film's resolution. Certainly, Alice's relationship with David is different from anything she has known before; their affection is openly and reciprocally expressed. Alice becomes insistent about her own needs; at one point, with the relationship at a crisis, Alice demands and wins from David a concession related to her desire to move on to Monterey. David agrees that if she wishes to leave, he will sell his ranch and accompany her. Yet there is also the annoying

Robert De Niro and Martin Scorsese on the set of *Taxi Driver*

The "death loft" scene from *Who's That Knocking at My Door*

Barbara Hershey and David Carradine in *Boxcar Bertha*

J.R. (Harvey Keitel) contemplating the fires of Hell in *Mean Streets*

Ellen Burstyn, Alfred Lutter, and Kris Kristofferson in *Alice Doesn't Live Here Anymore*

An icon of isolation: Robert De Niro as Travis Bickle in *Taxi Driver*

(top): Liza Minnelli and Robert De Niro in *New York, New York*; (bottom): The Band on stage in *The Last Waltz*

Robert De Niro as Jake La Motta in *Raging Bull*

Mirror images: Rupert (Robert De Niro) and Jerry (Jerry Lewis) during a fantasy scene from *The King of Comedy*

(top): Griffin Dunne and Rosanna Arquette in *After Hours*;
(bottom): Rosanna Arquette and Nick Nolte in "Life Lessons"

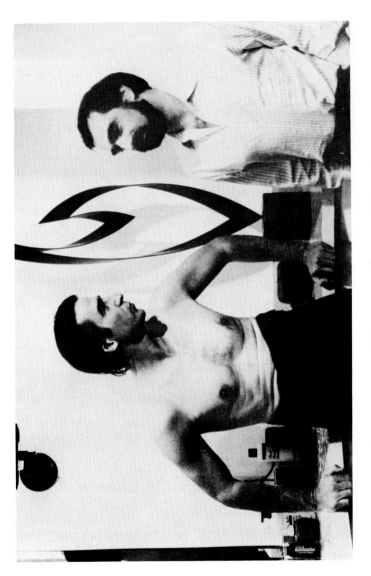

Sam Waterston and Scorsese on the set of *Mirror, Mirror*

Tom Cruise and Paul Newman in *The Color of Money*

Willem Dafoe as Jesus in *The Last Temptation of Christ*

Joe Pesci, Paul Sorvino, Robert De Niro, and Ray Liotta as the wise guys of *GoodFellas*

Robert De Niro and Nick Nolte in *Cape Fear*

Daniel Day-Lewis and Michelle Pfeiffer in *The Age of Innocence*

suspicion that Alice is the same person that she has always been. She is still strongly dependent on a man for emotional support, regardless of how liberated in attitude that man might be. What's more, it is important to note that as her relationship with David develops, Alice progressively gives up the idea of working on her own as a singer. Granted that her voice is rather poor, and that a repudiation of this aspiration may reflect a mature evaluation of her talents; yet we can also view her abandonment of her wish as a sacrifice of her ambition.

The essential problem with *Alice Doesn't Live Here Anymore* is that the film communicates a semblance of moral progress while what it actually catalogues is a story of spiritual inertia. Strictly speaking, Alice has merely substituted one life, meaningless without a man, for another in which she is as emotionally dependent as before. In this respect, the film invites comparison with Paul Mazursky's *An Unmarried Woman*. The Mazursky film's female protagonist, Erica (Jill Clayburgh), is similarly uprooted by a cataclysmic event: her husband leaves her, and she graduates from a flawed marriage to a relationship with a man (Alan Bates' Saul) who seems to treat her (as David treats Alice) as an equal. Both Alice and Erica are portrayed as having important relationships with strong-minded children who create conflicts with their mothers' new love interests.

At both films' ends, we are left with images of these women which suggest, not freedom, but an ambiguous struggle, one characterized by neither independence nor servitude. Erica is last seen maneuvering Saul's large painting down the street; she seems at once both decisive (her attempt to steer the painting along the street) and powerless (the way that the wind buffets her). Alice is last seen walking towards the goal that she identified after Donald's death: Monterey. Unfortunately, this mythical destination is now only a sign for the Monterey filling station. To further undermine the sense of Alice's progress, Alice's moving away from the camera is photographed with a telephoto lens that collapses the perspective, making it seem as if she is getting nowhere.

Ultimately, despite the feeling of satisfactory closure that the ends of these films engender, neither *An Unmarried Woman* nor *Alice* leaves us with a picture of a woman in control of her life. While both films chart a progress from oppression towards something better, neither shows its heroine getting what she really wants, and must be viewed as representations of the period in which they were filmed, a time of change characterized by a searching for new goals but, unfortunately, not necessarily an attainment of them.[2]

NOTES

1.   Scorsese previously used this frame-within-a-frame technique in *Italian American*.   At the end of this short film, the director freeze-frames a shot of his mother, reduces it in size, has the shot change to a nostalgic sepia tone, and insets it within the film's full-sized frame. Given *Italian American*'s wonderful evocation of the Scorsese family's past, which is visually captured in family stills, this metamorphosis of Catherine Scorsese into yet another family portrait brilliantly situates her in the familial context as a chromo of Italian-American life.

2.   The fact that Alice has set for herself a goal which she never reaches suggests a structural and thematic linkage between *Alice* and *Raging Bull*.   Although in the latter film the protagonist's goal is not consciously defined (nor is his inability to reach it a willing act, as it partially is for Alice), the notion of frustrated expectations is nonetheless similarly expressed in both films. This notion of delayed achievement assumes additional form in *Raging Bull*'s scene involving postponed ejaculation.

        One other notable similarity between *Alice* and *Raging Bull* is that in each film the central character moves from one heterosexual relationship to another, thinking that some form of progress is being made when, as is made clear to the audience, no substantial difference in the character's consciousness exists as a result of the change. Instead, as we discover, both Alice and Jake merely repeat with their new partners virtually all of the patterns of behavior that they manifested with their original mates.

Chapter Five

GOD'S LONELY MAN

Of the Scorsese films that feature Robert De Niro, it is *Taxi Driver* (1976) that commands the most respect. None of the other De Niro/Scorsese collaborations partakes of the strange inner logic and ineluctability that make *Taxi Driver* a true classic. De Niro's Travis Bickle is on a far greater and more profound journey (in this case, through the city's Hellish landscape) than any of the other characters that he has portrayed.

Essentially, Travis is in search of complete spiritual redemption, which the film shows as achievable only through violence. What distinguishes Travis is his desire to express verbally and understand intellectually exactly what is driving him. In attempting to reach such answers (which he does partially through keeping a diary, the only De Niro/Scorsese character self-conscious enough to do so), he becomes not only the mythic individual on a symbolic quest that the film makes him out to be, but a self-reflective figure whose thoughtfulness wins him a significant amount of audience identification and sympathy.

This achievement of sympathy is especially interesting because it occurs despite the normal reactions one might expect from an audience. After all, Travis is a seriously disturbed man who performs acts of gross physical violence in answer to a nameless and barely expressed calling. *Taxi Driver*'s black-joke ending has Travis elevated to the status of cultural hero; he is depicted by the media as a valiant crusader—the lone taxi driver battling the bad gangsters. This resolution is both ironic and improbable, since it seems doubtful that, given Travis's outlandish outfit and overstocked arsenal, the police would have found acceptable the newspaper-touted notion of Travis as a simple do-gooder engaged in a vendetta against evil. Nor does it seem probable that the Secret Service agent at the Palantine rally whom

Travis belittles would not have recognized in the newspaper photos of Travis the aberrant individual whom he had encountered earlier.

Taxi Driver's ending is given a further twist when we realize that Travis's initial target for violence is presidential candidate Charles Palantine, to whom Travis transfers his hostility after Betsy (Cybill Shepherd) refuses to see him again. Had Travis been successful in carrying out his original plan, he would have been an assassin, not a hero.

Unlike a similarly structured blow-out film such as *Straw Dogs*, *Taxi Driver* is unique in that a number of the film's victims do not seem to deserve their ends. Certainly, we can fairly easily dismiss the deaths of two men involved in Iris' prostitution: the mafioso and the sleazy apartment caretaker; these are, after all, character types who traditionally earn their usually horrible deaths. But the shooting of Harvey Keitel's Sport (who, as Iris points out, is not detaining her against her will) and the apparent killing of the black youth who holds up a delicatessen (a murder jointly carried out by Travis and the delicatessen's owner) seem out of proportion to these characters' offenses.

In fact, *Taxi Driver*'s entire attitude towards non-whites consists of a curious fascination with cultural "outsiders" along with a dread and anxiety that both attract and repel us at the same time. The film's sympathetic black taxi driver is surely a benign character, as are the black youths seen on the "American Bandstand" television show that Travis watches at home. Yet countering these impressions are the tough-looking blacks who frequent the Belmore Cafeteria (where the cab drivers meet), and the chain-bedecked black youth who brazenly struts past Travis outside the cafeteria.

Can we also ignore our ambiguous feelings about Sport, a reprehensible character to be sure, but a figure who despite his pimping and unctuous mannerisms elicits (for what must be described as basically comic reasons, given his outrageous clothes and haircut and the apparent glee with which Keitel attacks the part) an appreciable amount of sympathy as well?

An essential point to remember is that Sport and Travis are quite similar characters. Each one exploits Iris (Jodie Foster) for his own purposes. Sport tries to keep Iris docile and submissive so that he can continue to derive money from her prostitution, while Travis uses her as the excuse for giving in to his homicidal tendencies. Under the guise of saving her from a life that he views as corrupt (although there is no reason to believe that the deaths of Sport, the caretaker, and the mafioso were necessary to effect Iris' release), Travis goes on a murderous spree.

It would appear that Travis needs to achieve some form of moral and psychological blindness to the essential harmlessness of his "enemies" in order to perform his violent acts. The imaginary opponent to whom he speaks when practicing his gunmanship ("You talking to me; well, who the Hell else are you talking to?") and the painted-on figures at which he shoots on the rifle range are inhuman targets that he must treat as adversaries simply because there is no real, recognizable human enemy in the film on whom he can blame the city's corruption.[1] Like Charles Palantine, who misrepresents the true operation of politics (his "We are the people" slogan seems to suggest that people can directly influence politics when in fact his entire campaign, which sells him like a consumer product, only points up the deceptions inherent in the political process),[2] Travis oversimplifies the life that he sees in the city. Admittedly, much of what Travis views is sordid and objectionable; the city does (in Travis's words) seem to be "an open sewer," but its nastiness does not derive from any one source.

Through a process of narrowing, by means of which his goals become more and more modest (saving the city is reduced to saving voters from Palantine, which finally becomes saving Iris from her captors), Travis, like a darkly-conceived Don Quixote, works hard at creating objectionable windmills at which to tilt in order to justify his own directionless existence. What is most regrettable in *Taxi Driver* is not New York's corruption but the corruption of a man who can only find peace through violence, and who feels compelled to create search-and-destroy missions (a pattern of behavior doubtless stemming from his Marine training) in order to give meaning to his life. The only difference that really exists between Travis and ourselves is that Travis acts on his compulsions instead of suffering in silence.

Travis conceives of himself as being on a divine mission; as he puts it, he wants to see "a real rain come and wash all this scum off the streets." By this point in the film we have already heard Travis mention that at the end of his work shift he has to "clean the come off the back seat; some nights, I clean off the blood." In his concern with what he considers necessary cleansings, one can see how Travis has already to a degree prepared himself for the role of the city's deliverer from evil.[3] The fact that throughout the film, despite the garishly lit shots that characterize it, Travis's cab is often covered with glistening droplets of water suggests that its occupant—inside his chariot, within which like a dutiful Charon he ferries his passengers across New York's deadly streets—is a man suited to the role of liberator from corruption.

Yet Travis is in no sense represented as a divine deliverer. The shots towards the film's beginning of his cab slowly emerging from sewer steam[4] suggest that he is, additionally, a messenger from Hell. However, since Travis (along with all of New York's occupants) is himself in Hell, it seems appropriate that it be one of the underworld's inhabitants who, in rebellion, attempts to effect a change.[5]

On his initial appearance at Iris' apartment, Travis arrives, not in the guise of a knight in shining armor (a role that the impeccably-coiffed and -dressed, white-maned Palantine/paladin affects), but in casual dress. He offers Iris financial help if she will leave the city, thereby attempting to use the spoils of corruption—the money he earns from driving the "spooks, whores, and junkies" whom he ferries around—to fight corruption.

Much like the lone cowboys in the Old West, where every man with a gun was a law unto himself, Travis is a solitary man riding shotgun through the night, a self-appointed marshal cruising the streets for trouble and righting wrongs (e.g., the grocery store holdup, the supposed oppression of Iris) wherever he sees them.[6] Like all of the other characters whom De Niro plays in Scorsese films, Travis is isolated. "I'm God's lonely man," he writes in his diary. He is a man not only incapable of establishing and maintaining relationships with other people but one who, for indeterminable reasons, is constituted differently from those around him. Alone and left to his own devices, Travis must construct and live by his own moral code. *Taxi Driver* leads us to identify isolation as the catalyst for Travis's self-destructive impulses.[7] In essence, because he is unable to achieve effective communication with other people, Travis is left without the guidance of human experience. As a consequence, his distorted notions about life (he derives his knowledge of love from the pornographic movies he attends, and his knowledge of human interaction from the soap operas he watches) are allowed to develop untempered by the attitudes and opinions of others.

The film may in one sense be read as a tract warning us of the dangers involved when communication among people fails. There is evidence of this in the non-sequitur discussions among the cab drivers; the cliche-ridden dialogues Travis has with Betsy and Iris; and Travis's pointless talk with Wizard (Peter Boyle), in which the only clear statement Travis can make about his condition is, "I got some bad ideas in my head." Wizard's offered rejoinder? "Get drunk . . . get laid . . . you're all right." Travis's tag name tells it all: Travis Bickle is a man destined to travel towards argumentative (bickle/bicker) confrontations. Although as a cab driver Travis takes people everywhere, the only location towards which he is himself heading is a place where he can play out his self-styled Armageddon.

Our reactions to Travis are highly ambiguous. The self-justified loner, the man who not only carries out the law but *is* the law, has a revered place in our national mythology. Often, as in films such as *High Noon*, the lawman becomes the law's last representative, with the rest of the townspeople cowed into submission to tyrannical outlaws whose self-assurance brands them as superior to the equivocal citizens. Only the man who is upright and pure (thus Travis's purification rites before attempting to shoot Palantine: "No more pills, no more bad food, no more destroyers of my body") can hope to successfully oppose urban corruption.

Correlative to his belief in God ("I'm *God's* lonely man," my emphasis) is Travis's belief in the Hellish judgment that he thinks awaits him in response to his planned homicidal actions. In this respect Travis is like *Mean Streets'* Charlie, a comparison that highlights an essential point in the taxi driver's character. Charlie prepares for the Hell towards which he believes he is heading by thrusting his fingers into fire, as though he were already damned. Travis, though, conceives of fire not as the stuff of damnation but as a purifier, which he uses to prepare for his divine mission; he holds his fist in a flame to steel himself for the pain of his mission, and burns Betsy's flowers to free himself from emotional attachments. Charlie sees Hell as the place where he will spend eternity; Travis views Hell as a purgatorial prerequisite to salvation, a prelude to the peace that awaits him after he passes through the trials of the murder (or, as it turns out, murders) that he plans to commit. Like Jesus, he is ready to die (his note to Iris states in part, "When you read this I will be dead") and spend a few days in Hell so that he can eventually attain Paradise. Charlie's indecisiveness consigns him to a Hell on earth; Travis believes that his decisive actions will allow him to transcend the city's Hell, which he apparently conceives of as reserved only for weak individuals. Thus, between *Mean Streets* and *Taxi Driver*, Scorsese's view of violence has subtly changed; earlier, violence (e.g., Charlie's shooting) was a divine judgment on those who wavered; now it is a divine act that delivers one *beyond* judgment.

In setting Travis against the forces of evil, Scorsese places the audience in a moral double bind. Shall we applaud Travis's desire to do something about all of the filth in New York? After all, as *Taxi Driver* demonstrates, the traditional enforcers of the law, the police, seem ineffective in dealing with crime and violence (they only arrive on the scene after a crime has been committed). Or should we condemn him for his pointless, precipitous acts? The fact that De Niro makes Travis a relatively attractive character only makes our ability to achieve a resolution of these contrary impulses more difficult.

As a subtle prelude to the film's twist ending, scriptwriter Paul Schrader inserts a mild twist into the events preceding the blow-out. We have seen Travis approach Iris' apartment in relatively traditional garb; Travis's jeans and boots are part of the cowboy's familiar attire (indeed, Sport and the apartment building caretaker refer to him as "cowboy"). When Travis returns to mete out his own form of western-style justice, he appears with a mohawk-style haircut and, in the guise of an Indian, hands out vengeance to the cowboy types who have appropriated from him the land of essential innocence.

Travis has been witness to both Hell (the city's corruption) and Heaven (embodied in his vision of Betsy, who is seen dressed all in white: he views her as an angel of purity in the midst of corruption and writes of her, "She is alone; they cannot touch her"). Yet since in his present state he exists completely in neither realm, dwelling instead in a moral and spiritual limbo, he finds it impossible to make mature contact with a woman (as opposed to a young girl, like Iris) from either sphere. In the midst of debauchery, at a pornographic movie house, he tries to make a date with the woman behind the candy counter and, when rebuffed, childishly asks for "Jujubes, they last longer." Ultimately, he is just as unsuccessful with Betsy; his taking Betsy to an X-rated movie merely reflects his lack of experience with women.

Spurned by two women—one debased, one who is initially conceived of in terms of her purity—and repelled by the "whores, scum, and pussy" that he sees on the streets, Travis finds to his good fortune a street angel, part hooker, part (at least to him) virgin (as Travis says to Iris at one point, "This is nothing for a person to do . . . you're a young girl. You should be home now, you should be dressed up, you should be going out with boys") on whom he can concentrate his efforts. That the murders in the tenement apartment

house, and not the money he offers her to get out of the city, result in
Iris's safe return to her parents' home is only a further, minor twist to
the film's ironic ending. In essence, *Taxi Driver* demonstrates that
only violence, not money, will help Iris escape.

In any case, the money that Travis sends her in the mail is
tainted: it comes from his shepherding many disturbed people—the
businessman with the hooker, the man with the gun—around the city.
The twenty dollar bill that Sport tosses him, which Travis views as
more polluted than all of his other money, only gains Travis entrance
to the tenement for the final shoot-out, but does not effect Iris's release
(although its employment is a fine example of corruption being used
against itself), whereas the shoot-out *does* directly result in her being
returned to her parents. The film makes it clear that in contrast to
debased money, violence, judging by its positive effect, is something
pure.

Taxi Driver presents Travis as a rather pitiable figure.
Although Travis writes in his diary, "Listen you fuckers, you
screwheads, here is a man who would not take it anymore, a man who
stood up against the scum, the cunts, the dogs, the shit—here is
someone who stood up," Scorsese immediately follows this entry with
a shot of Travis lying on his bunk, first in an unnaturally stiff,
corpse-like position on his back, then on his side, curled into a
regressive fetal attitude.[8] He hardly qualifies as a self-assured
champion of justice. Again, the film's double bind emerges. In spite
of ourselves, we must admire Travis's ability to act on his beliefs, yet
Scorsese continually provides us with visual images that contradict this
tendency. Thus, the message derived from seeing Travis—in full battle
gear—curled up is that violence is an immature act. Such intentional
ambiguity only adds to the film's moral and psychological complexity.

Travis is similarly undeveloped when it comes to sexual
matters. The only way he can interact with Betsy is by trying to
impress her with his perceptiveness by telling her how lonely he knows
she really is. It is a testament to Betsy's basic naivete that she is
influenced by this absurdly conventional, tired rhetoric. Rejected by
Betsy and shocked by his isolation (even when associating with the
cabbies he seems distant and removed), Travis becomes a
mytho-maniac who embarks on a quest to revitalize the sterile New
York City wasteland.

Travis's view of women is also mythical; he conceives of only
two kinds of women: virgins and whores. Interestingly, Betsy and Iris

each assume both roles. Originally a vision of purity, Betsy is later viewed by Travis as a fallen woman deserving damnation both in this life ("You're in Hell") and the one to come ("You'll burn in Hell"). In a complementary fashion, Iris is first whore, then, when she rejoins her family, virgin once again. The complementarity of roles extends to Travis himself. When he first sees Betsy, Travis is the sullied man seeking redemption through a pure woman. With Iris, though, the woman is the one who is tainted, and the man assumes the role of the savior. Not at all interested in either a sexual or platonic relationship with Iris, Travis remains throughout the film on the periphery of male/female relations, always observing and desiring but never (not even in fantasies) participating.

Of course, one should not discount the appreciable sublimation in which Travis indulges during his preparation for his mission. Cinematographer Michael Chapman's camera lingers over the phallic length of the .44 magnum that Travis purchases from Andy (Steven Prince),[9] and there is clearly a significant degree of narcissism present in Travis's preparations for his upcoming encounter. Additionally, his conversations with his imaginary mirror image opponent, clashes from which he always emerges triumphant, doubtless appeal to Travis's sense of egotism.

The film's fateful foreshadowings (a trademark of Scorsese films with dark undercurrents, such as *Who's That Knocking at My Door* and *Mean Streets*), which are present here in the twenty dollar bill that Travis seems to be saving for some special event, the purchase of firearms, and the ritualistic burning of the flowers bought for Betsy, work to create an atmosphere of oppression. Particularly noteworthy is the feeling of inevitability communicated in two crucial scenes. Immediately preceding the scene in which Travis purchases guns from Andy, the film's soundtrack gives forth with repeated snare drum rolls, suggesting the militaristic, kamikaze aspects of Travis's impending mission (as his note to Iris indicates, he does not expect to return alive). Additionally, the drum rolls suggest the march to an execution, their repetition hinting that the unstoppable mechanism of fate has already been set in motion. This fateful aspect reappears in the subsequent scene in which Travis prepares to meet Palantine. Throughout this sequence, a clock is heard in the background, ominously ticking off the minutes that remain until the planned assassination. With the camera restlessly pacing back and forth past a corner of the table on which Travis is intently constructing his quick-draw device and converting his regular bullets into dum-dums, the sense of unease is further heightened.

The viewer should also note that Travis seems virtually destined to become involved in Iris' life. Indeed, she is twice accidentally thrust into his path before he seeks her out, thereby indicating that more than mere chance appears to be bringing them together. Travis first sees Iris when she enters his cab during an argument with Sport; later, in the company of a female friend, she steps in front of his cab and is almost run over. During her brunch with Travis, Iris entertains the notion of leaving New York for a commune (that is, if Travis will accompany her), which suggests that Travis represents for her a catalytic, curative force. This role precisely reflects the way that he views himself. Travis tries to save Betsy from boredom, to liberate Iris from oppression. The two women's equivalent status in his life is only further affirmed by Bernard Herrmann's astute use of the same romantic love theme to accompany many of the scenes in which they appear.

In response to Travis's failed attempt to verbalize his anxiety, Wizard—speaking more perceptively than he knows—points up the fact that man's fate, despite his efforts, is sealed. "You got no choice anyway," he says. Travis appropriates this notion of fate; in doing so, he attempts to lend teleological purpose to his plans. Incorrectly attributing his anxiety solely to seclusion, he writes, "Loneliness has followed me everywhere . . . there's no escape," although it's possible that he views his homicidal quest, which is a new idea to him, as a possible release from his alienation. However, as *Taxi Driver*'s end makes clear, there is not only no deviation from fate but no change in Travis as a result of his actions. He is destined to be alienated.

Narrating an entry into his diary, Travis states, "The days move along with regularity, over and over, one day indistinguishable from the next, a long, continuous chain. Then suddenly, there is change." Immediately after the word "change" we see Travis meeting Andy. The "change" for which Travis has been waiting (which is really less a change than the fulfillment of his fate) is the accessibility to the weapons that he needs to carry out his plans. What Travis represents as an implicit change for the better is actually an explicit turn for the worse: the purchase of guns by a man who has severe psychological problems.

When Andy first appears he is referred to as "easy Andy, a travelling salesman." Andy's nickname links him with Iris, who initially tells Travis that her name is "Easy," and who, like Andy, travels the streets meeting people to whom she sells her "goods." Sex (Iris) and death (the weapons that Andy sells) are here verbally linked.

The substitution of death-connoting objects (in particular, weapons) for acts of love (symbolized by the penis) is one of *Taxi Driver*'s most important aspects, a quality that can be seen to derive from similar attitudes in *Mean Streets*. In the present film, the symbolic replacement of the penis by the gun is initially established when one of Travis's fares (played by Scorsese) talks about what a .44 magnum "can do to a woman's pussy." The speaker is a man whose wife is cheating on him (appropriately, given the film's expression of fear of dark-skinned characters, with a black man; the fare refers to him as "a nigger"). It is therefore entirely fitting that Travis, who cannot successfully express himself sexually, first asks Andy if he has a .44 magnum. Given the absence in *Taxi Driver* of normal hetero-sexual relationships (the only characters who exhibit closeness are Sport and Iris in their dance together, yet the dance is obviously a ploy of Sport's to keep Iris in his stable; Wizard talks about having sex in the back seat of his cab with one of his customers—almost certainly a fantasy), we must conclude that the men in the film who have guns cannot successfully express themselves sexually in any other way.

Just as the gun takes the place of the penis, violence takes the place of tenderness and communication. Overt aggression is thus depicted as the response of individuals who not only are incapable of achieving human closeness but cannot tolerate seeing it enjoyed by others. Consequently, when Travis evaluates the .25 Colt automatic that Andy is showing him, he sights it out the window at a couple seated on a park bench. Later, Travis will again thrust his way into the middle of other people's relationships and fantasize breaking up their interaction, as when he aims the magnum at a black couple whom he watches dancing together on "American Bandstand,"[10] and when he uses his hand as a pretend gun to shoot a couple in a pornographic movie that he attends.[11]

Even after the film's final murders, when Travis's deadly passions are supposedly (at least for a time) quelled, he still cannot jettison this hostile attitude, reinvoking the hand-as-gun gesture (to which he resorts after finding that all of his guns are empty and that he cannot therefore really shoot himself) by bringing his right hand to his temple and, index finger extended, firing three imaginary shots into his brain. By this point in the film, having accomplished his task, Travis is apparently ready to commit suicide by turning some of his formerly externalized aggressions against himself.

Additionally, we should note that the black cabdriver and Wizard seem to recognize Travis's potential for violence. Both call Travis "killer," references that occur within two minutes of each other and which bracket the sequence in which Travis directs an angry, hostile stare at a black youth who struts past the Belmore Cafeteria. Travis's already-noted hostile attitude towards blacks—affirmed in the "killer" reference, exemplified in his stare, and soon to take concrete form in the delicatessen shooting—is eventually given full expression when, at the film's end, he takes vengeance against the three "dark" characters (the swarthy Sport, the dark caretaker, the unctuous mafioso) whom he has identified as his enemies. Combined with the film's moody pacing (slow and, in tandem with the plot, ominous), intentionally garish colors (blood-like reds and threatening blacks predominate), and washed-out lighting, these powerful aspects draw the viewer into *Taxi Driver*'s menacing urban milieu.

Even in the midst of humorous interplay, *Taxi Driver* sets up morose foreshadowings. The game that Betsy's co-worker Tom (Albert Brooks) plays—which involves trying to light a match one-handed while pretending that three fingers on the left hand are missing—does more than implicate him in the film's hand-as-gun-as- penis schema. The game not only involves an implicit castration wish, thus characterizing the essence of Tom's essential sexuality, but bears homicidal fruit when Travis first shoots three fingers off the tenement caretaker's right hand. Then, when the caretaker—having followed Travis upstairs—attacks him in Iris's room, the incident is, in effect, repeated. Travis impales the man's left hand with a knife, an action that causes three of the caretaker's fingers involuntarily to curl inward, as though they had disappeared.[12]

Travis repays Sport in kind. When he is first with Iris, she unsuccessfully attempts to fellate him (as Sport earlier promises, "You can come in her mouth . . . "). Travis figuratively turns this sexual trick against Sport; when he shoots Sport in the stomach, Travis tells him to "suck on this," the reference thereby reinvoking for us the gun's substitution for the male organ.

Taxi Driver's music also anticipates its shocking conclusion. In a rare, self-reflexive homage to his own work, composer Bernard Herrmann reprises the three-note murder theme from *Psycho* to anticipate some homicidal activity. In *Taxi Driver*, this music appears immediately before the delicatessen hold-up and shooting (itself visually anticipated in the hostility Travis shows towards the black teenagers he watches on "American Bandstand") and during the film's final credit sequence when, accompanying the film's last image (a washed-out, overexposed shot of a city street as seen from Travis's cab), the theme is reprised, indicating that although we are presumably in the safe area beyond the film's action, the possibility of unpredictable violence still exists.[13]

Taxi Driver's ending clearly indicates whether or not Travis's violence has delivered him from his anxieties and their homicidal effects. While it is true that by the film's conclusion Travis is no longer obsessed with Betsy or her damnation, there is no reason to believe that he is free from his fixation on corruption and evil. After a calm ride with Betsy, Travis pulls his cab away from the curb and once again begins to drift though through the urban night. The garish city lights reflect in his rear view mirror; the editing is smooth, deceptively lulling, until Scorsese introduces a discordant musical sting and gives us three rapid, alternate-angle shots of Travis looking at himself in his rear view mirror—an action/reaction trio (with Travis obviously still playing the "You talking to me?" game, which was also conducted in front of a mirror) which chillingly indicates that the homicidal ride is far from being over.

NOTES

1. Scorsese has addressed the issue of a tendency to violence which, undirected, is ultimately turned against one's self (present in *Taxi Driver* in Travis's willingness to commit suicide at the film's end and his apparent, self-destructive ability to institute new, perilous vendettas in the future) in his short film *The Big Shave* (1967-1968), which concerns a young man who can't stop shaving until he cuts his own throat. The short's soundtrack is highly ironic, since Scorsese uses Bunny Berrigan's version of "I Can't Get Started" not only to provide a cutting rhythm for the film and to act as a romantic/sexual counterpoint to *The Big Shave*'s violence (the latter characteristic, the yoking of impulses towards love and death, is present in all of Scorsese's films) but also ironically to play off against the fact that the problem for the young man in the film is not that "he can't get started," but that he simply cannot stop. This parable of overt violence unleashed against one's self (violence which ultimately ends in one's own destruction) ends with the title "Viet 67," thus confirming the film's status as a statement about the essentially self-

destructive aspect of the United States' military presence in Southeast Asia.

2.   Scorsese emphasizes Palantine's essential artificiality by repeatedly giving us shots of the candidate that cut off his head, as though the politician is merely a brainless puppet mechanically and incessantly mouthing platitudes.

3.   Scorsese seems to support the view of the city as essentially corrupt in an interesting shot during a scene at the cafeteria. Travis has just dropped two Alka Seltzers into a glass of water (he probably suffers from indigestion in addition to sleeplessness, although one wonders how the previous condition is affected by his putting cheap liquor over his breakfast cereal). As the tablets begin to fizz, Scorsese zooms in on the contents of the glass, and the camera discovers a tiny, but nonetheless recognizable, speck of dirt, as though to suggest that even in curative draughts there are signs of pollution and corruption, aspects of the city that Travis, in his blind quest for some form of revenge against the urban monster, opposes.

4.   Appropriately, it is from such steam at the end of the title sequence that Scorsese's name emerges, first in white, then slowly fading into a blood-red color that presages the violence to come.

        Scorsese likes to present himself this way, as a lover of violence. As early as *The Big Shave*, he employs a fade to red, which occurs after a significant amount of bloodletting and before the end credits, to emphasize the shocking nature of violence.

5.   Despite its supposedly laudatory purpose (the newspapers claim that he was trying to save Iris), Travis's homicidal outburst at the film's end will itself contribute to the view of New York as a dangerous place to live, a city where violence is often used against violence. Nevertheless, Travis does have a solution to the city's filth: "flush it right down the fucking toilet."

        Travis's view of the city as debased is quite traditional. Frank Lloyd Wright, quoted in Susan Sontag's *Illness as Metaphor* (New York: Vintage Books, 1978), referred to cities as cancerous blights: "To look at the cross-section of any plan of a big city is to look at the section of a fibrous tumor" (pp. 72-73). While Travis's reference to the city as a sewer emulates this view, an even stronger link with Wright's astute perspective is present in Travis's statement that he thinks he has "stomach cancer," an attitude doubtless reflecting an internalization of the city's inherent sickness and corruption. In his dual impulses towards both sickness (taking drugs to work longer hours, gulping aspirin for recurrent headaches, putting liquor on his cereal) and health (swearing off all drugs, adopting a rigid plan of body-building and regeneration), Travis reveals that he represents a typical city in microcosm.

6.   Of course, it is possible that Travis wants to kill Palantine because he recognizes him as a "wrong," as a hypocrite. Yet given his endorsement of Palantine's campaign, offered while he drives Palantine to a hotel, and Travis's hostile reaction to Betsy's rejecting him, it is likely that he wants to kill the politician solely as a way of hurting the woman who hurt him.

7.   Although isolation is clearly a major cause of Travis's imbalances, we must nevertheless acknowledge that Travis derives some sort of benefit from acting alone. His self-styled vendetta against corruption becomes a satisfying fight precisely because Travis wills it to be so. In light of the film's end, Travis actually seems to thrive in the big-city environment; removed from the city and its threatening atmosphere, he would doubtless languish in the suffocating peacefulness of the commune towards which Iris would steer him.

8.   Travis's only rival for Betsy's affections—Betsy's fellow campaign worker, Tom—is similarly stunted in his personal growth, a characteristic communicated most clearly when, in what he means to be a humorous riposte, he tells Betsy that "I'll *play* the male in this relationship" (my emphasis).

9.   The stand-out performance of Steven Prince in the role of gun salesman Andy should here be noted. Prince's comically speeded-up verbal delivery, and the way he blandly sells Travis on the various weapons he shows him ("That's a beauty," he says, going on to state with unintentional comic irony, "I deal high quality goods to the right people") are delightful. Interestingly, despite his unquestioning willingness to sell the guns to Travis, Andy nevertheless realizes the weapons' potential for misuse. Referring to a Colt .25, Andy states, "It's a nice little gun, it's a beautiful little gun; it [the chamber] holds six rounds, if you're dumb enough to put a round in."

Prince's portrayal brings up an important consideration: the nature of the humor that *Taxi Driver* uses. In one sense the entire film may be taken as a black comedy; Wizard's asinine analysis of Travis's condition, the sequence with Andy, Travis's luncheonette discussion with Iris about horoscope signs and communes, and the film's ironic ending support this view.

Further insights into Prince's personality may be gleaned from Scorsese's short film *American Boy: A Profile of Steven Prince* (1978), film number two (after *Italian American*) in what the director planned as a six-film cycle of works about various nationalities. Oddly enough, Prince chooses in the film to relate a remark made by his father which has to do with the kind of attitude towards weaponry exhibited in *Taxi Driver*. Prince quotes his father as saying, "Never point a gun at anyone unless you plan to shoot. Never shoot unless you plan to kill." The words are strongly applicable to Travis's initial feints with his gun, which *Taxi Driver*'s viewer soon realizes are practice moves for his later actual use of the weapon.

10.   The scene involving the pretend shooting of the black dancers occurs immediately after the delicatessen holdup sequence, during which Travis shot a black youth. It would appear, then, that Travis's appetite for racial vengeance has been whetted by his first homicidal experience, and that he is now searching for a new way to appease it.

11.   In a daring move, Scorsese later reprises the gun-as-penis symbology. Watching a television soap opera scene about a couple's marital difficulties, Travis again reacts negatively and with violence to heterosexual intimacy, first sublimating his sexual desire by sitting with the magnum's barrel jutting out like a penis between his legs, then directly expressing his hostility and frustration by intentionally knocking over the television set.

12.   The sirens heard in the background when Travis and Iris enter her building during their first encounter silently reappear after the shoot-out when a patrol car pulls up outside the building thus complementing the sense of fulfilled inevitability created here.

13.   However, Herrmann did not intend that his three-note theme end the film. Instead, as his score for *Taxi Driver* indicates, Herrmann wanted the final title sequence to conclude with a symphonic resolution of the theme's discordance. Apparently perceiving that such an assertion of order in the face of the film's chaos was inappropriate, Scorsese eliminated this musical conclusion. One can only speculate about whether the strong-willed Herrmann, who died before the film's completion, would have sanctioned such editing of his work. In any case, students of *Taxi Driver* can evaluate the film's music by purchasing the long-out-of-print (and now reissued) soundtrack, which is available on Sweet Thunder records (distributed by Arista Records, 1776 Broadway, New York, N.Y. 10019).

     Taxi Driver's most notable Hitchcock cross reference, though, is Scorsese's use of an extended, slow-motion backward tracking shot out of the murder room, down the tenement's stairs, and out into the street. The shot is, apparently, an intentional homage to the virtually identical backward tracing shot (also away from a "murder room") that occurs approximately midway through Hitchcock's *Frenzy* (1972).

Chapter Six

HELLO TO NEW YORK; GOODBYE TO THE BAND

It should come as little surprise that Scorsese was strongly interested in two musical projects—*New York, New York* (1977) and *The Last Waltz* (1978)—especially when one considers not only his involvement as supervising editor of Michael Wadleigh's *Woodstock* but his strong reliance on music in most of his films. Given the casting of Robert De Niro as Jimmy Doyle, a comically obsessed saxophone player who comes into conflict with authority and a rather conventionally-minded lover (Liza Minnelli's Francine Evans), *New York, New York* seems like a logical outgrowth of the approach to characterization present in *Mean Streets* and *Taxi Driver*. How much difference, after all, is there between Jimmy and Travis Bickle? Both are intense, single-minded individuals. Travis would no sooner give up his taxicab, which ferries him magically through Hell, than Jimmy would give up his saxophone. As Jimmy says to Francine at one point when she questions his playing in Harlem every night, "Do you want me to smash this thing (his saxophone) against the building? Is that what you want me to do?" Jimmy's instrument provides him with the means of therapeutically working out his aggressions in the same way that Travis' toying with (and ultimate expression of) violence provides him with a means of passage through the underworld of pimps and pushers.

New York, New York's opening titles give us a clue to the violence-prone, nether-world forces beneath the film's veneer when we see that, as in *Taxi Driver* (which begins with shots of Travis' cab emerging from subterranean steam), its director's name appears, not in pink like *New York, New York*'s other titles, but in red. The underworld suggestion here—one reflected in the film's protagonist, Jimmy Doyle—is most obvious. It is clear that for all of his kidding and comic patter, Jimmy is like a drug addict in constant withdrawal, whose only means of escape from his own excessive behavior and the straight

62

world around him is through his palliative: music. Like Travis, Jimmy requires attention and gets it; Travis wins acclaim through his violence, Jimmy through his playing. Travis and Jimmy may blow slightly different tunes played on different "instruments," yet each needs some form of acceptance, some indication that his efforts bear recognizable fruit (Travis through "saving" Iris; Jimmy through commercial success with his group) to pour balm on his cruel inner fires.

Jimmy is a likable but often annoying fanatic. The fact that he elicits our sympathy and commands our respect (regardless of how great a musician he is, he is still a poor human being) affirms once again the manner in which Scorsese can have us sympathize with a character whom we might normally condemn. Equally responsible for Jimmy's acceptability is his portrayal by Robert De Niro. By now, students of Scorsese's work, and viewers of film in general, have come to appreciate De Niro's extraordinary talents. We enjoy his antics, even when he is portraying characters who are reprehensible (e.g. *Raging Bull*'s Jake La Motta and *Cape Fear*'s Max Cady) or annoyingly vulgar (e.g. *King of Comedy*'s Rupert Pupkin).

De Niro's performance, and the atmosphere of barely repressed, dangerous aggression that he creates around him, would lead one to believe that what we have in *New York, New York* is a successful film. Yet *New York, New York* seems more like a good idea for a film than a well-realized production. While there is much to enjoy in *New York, New York*—especially the opening thirty minutes, as the Jimmy Doyle character is given room to develop—the film's rags-to-riches love story seems for the most part rather dull and lifeless. Though Scorsese obviously wished to resurrect this classic formula and give it a new twist by using strongly contemporary actors like De Niro (whose delivery of comic lines is masterful), he detracts from the production's verve by using Liza Minnelli more for her Judy Garland qualities (the large eyes, the big-voiced delivery of songs) than for the contemporary appeal the actress had at the time.

Moreover, the conventional aspects of the production, especially during its second half, overshadow whatever vibrancy De Niro and Minnelli bring to the film. *New York, New York*'s production numbers are for the most part enjoyable, and the title number is especially good, although it amounts to little more than a filmed nightclub rendition of the song. However, in his desire to pay homage to forties musicals, Scorsese allows his usual good judgment to be put in abeyance by including (and restoring to the initially cut release version) the appalling "Happy Endings" number, which appeals neither as an original production sequence nor as a tribute. The number is best summed up by Jimmy Doyle (who sees it in Francine's latest film) when he tells Francine he has seen "Sappy Endings." Sappy is certainly the word for it; the woefully sentimental spirit that the sequence embodies ultimately infects the whole movie, thereby defusing this hopeful and energetic film.

Nevertheless, we should be reluctant to completely dismiss *New York, New York* when we consider the manner in which it fits into Scorsese's canon. What we're again seeing is the exemplification of conflict in the lives of characters with whom Scorsese seems intimately involved. These characters' association with the engaging music that they create makes it plain that they are inspired, and when a character in Scorsese's work is inspired, we need to look for a rationale for this characteristic's presence. In *New York, New York*, what we see is that both Jimmy and Francine have been given gifts of musical creativity that represent both a blessing and a curse: a blessing in that these gifts give them the pleasure of creation and lift them up to fame; a curse in that these gifts remove them from the ordinary realm, condemning them to lead idiosyncratic lives within which a fulfilling romantic relationship seem impossible to maintain. Francine may be a bit more willing than Jimmy to subordinate her talent to a family role, but both of them seem doomed to exemption from domestic happiness. The Scorsese schema again seems plain: like Jesus in *The Last Temptation of Christ*, when you're chosen, you're condemned to be set apart. All of Scorsese's characters must live out the terms of their own individual ministries; it's only individuals such as *Alice Doesn't Live Here Anymore*'s Alice Hyatt who can approach a degree of satisfaction that is, in any case, achieved by virtue of a melancholy compromise with one's true desires.

If *New York, New York* is a well-intentioned failure, by what designation may we refer to *The Last Waltz*? An interview/concert film focusing on The Band's farewell performance, *The Last Waltz* is unsuccessful in distinguishing itself from many other concert films. The audience is given technically competent, filmed versions of many Band songs, as well as views of various performers (among them Joni Mitchell, Neil Young, Bob Dylan, Dr. John, and Van Morrison) who stopped by to participate in the proceedings, but the footage is in no sense different from the type of music event coverage to which we have been exposed in films like *Woodstock, Monterey Pop, A Film About Jimi Hendrix*, etc., except for one small but significant detail: the virtual absence of any shots of the audience.

It is traditional in films of this type for the director to give us views of the appreciative crowd. Perhaps it was in reaction against what had become a cliche that Scorsese decided to show us virtually nothing of the concert goers. Yet a more comprehensive explanation for this approach suggests itself: namely, that Scorsese was not predominantly interested in the concert as an event for the audience's entertainment, but as a symbolic act that had meaning for him as a filmmaker.

Why else would Scorsese have gone to the trouble of making the film at all? Even if he were a fanatical devotee of The Band's music, one would think that he would therefore have concentrated more on the concert and devoted less screen time to the musings of the Band's lead guitarist (and apparent spokesman) Robbie Robertson.

Given the amount of footage devoted to Robertson, the film might just as well have been titled *Robbie Robertson Speaks*. Given Robertson's self-conscious posturings on stage during the concert, and his back-stage ramblings, the film virtually constitutes a vehicle for his musical and verbal skills. It is difficult to avoid the negative impression that Robertson makes on the viewer, since little of his lead guitar work in the film is outstanding, while his off-stage reminiscences are not very different from the kinds of stories that any veteran musician could tell.

It is likely that what Scorsese saw in Robertson was an eerie reflection of himself. Both Scorsese and Robertson are leaders of groups: Scorsese coordinates and directs the activities of various professionals on a film set; Robertson encourages cohesion among The Band's members. Each man is thus involved in preparing others (and sometimes himself) for performances. Moreover, as their groups' leaders, both Scorsese and Robertson expose themselves to the potential negative criticism that a bad performance (be it a concert, a record, or a film) may occasion.

It may be that in allowing Robertson to give in to his self-aggrandizing impulses, Scorsese somehow exorcises his own, and that through Robertson, Scorsese achieves some tempering of the hubris that being the main force behind million-dollar films may occasion. Perhaps what Scorsese sees in Robertson's incessant talking, then, is a part of himself that he would prefer to tone down.

As the title indicates, *The Last Waltz* is about endings; this concert is indeed a goodbye. In the film it is, literally, The Band that is being dispatched, but what we symbolically see in *The Last Waltz* is a whole era of rock music that is disappearing. True, The Band's playing is lively, but the same cannot be said for their guest artists, who seem for the most part to be a rather tired, uninspired bunch. Joni Mitchell and Muddy Waters escape this judgment (Dr. John's set is interesting, but we've seen this identical act numerous times before), but Neil Young, Paul Butterfield, Van Morrison, and Bob Dylan bring very little to their performances. Young seems distracted during the singing of "Helpless"; Paul Butterfield's harmonica playing is dull and uninspired; it is all Van Morrison can do to work up a bit of energy for his song. As for Dylan, while his drawn-out vowels and nasal twang delivery may be suitable for some songs, it is inappropriate for the beautiful folk song "Baby Let Me Follow You Down," which is further ruined by the singer's electric guitar back-up.

Dylan's other offering, "Forever Young," is significant only in the choice of song. *The Last Waltz* is clearly a film about a group of once-young musicians who have reached an impasse; one only remains "forever young" in dreams. Appropriately, the marquee of the Winterland Theatre, where *The Last Waltz* was filmed, comments on the whole situation. Most of the letters in the theatre's sign—like the inspirational lights of many of the performers we see in the film—have burned out.

Perhaps there is a warning in *The Last Waltz* that ultimately constitutes its basic message. Robertson notes towards the film's end that music is a hard road. The Band had sixteen years of it. "The road has taken many of the great ones," says Robertson. "It's a goddamned impossible way of life." It may be that in this observation Scorsese sees a parallel with his own work, itself as emotionally rewarding and spiritually demanding as The Band's. As Robertson implies, maybe it's time to stop pressing one's luck and quit. Perhaps such a fateful conclusion also expresses Martin Scorsese's fear that if he presses too hard, the entertainment road will figuratively kill his talents as well. Ultimately, then, *The Last Waltz* is a testament, not only to the end of a musical period, but also to the beginning of a grim reflectiveness in the work of its director.

Chapter Seven

THE ANIMAL

Raging Bull (1980) presents the viewer with a perplexing dilemma. While the film is clearly one of Scorsese's most ambitious works, employing stunning black-and-white cinematography and incorporating Robert De Niro's brilliant portrayal of fighter Jake La Motta, it nevertheless represents the first time that Scorsese has chosen as his central character an individual who is predominantly unsympathetic.

Such a situation would not prove so troublesome (after all, many films have dealt with objectionable protagonists) were it not that the structure of the film, as well as its textual epilogue, indicate that what we are supposed to see in *Raging Bull* is the progress of an unreflective, unself-conscious character towards wisdom and self-awareness.[1] Unfortunately, while this is clearly the film's intention, it is at variance with its effects.

The disjunction in the film between Jake's desires and the social forces that prescribe acceptable behavior is central to *Raging Bull*'s action. The problem with *Raging Bull*, though, is that we are never able to view Jake as a character who is either divinely tormented or redeemed through some resolution of the conflicting demands of the word and the flesh. Moreover, although Jake realizes that there is something wrong with him, he is unable to locate the basis of his dilemma.

Raging Bull begins in 1964; Jake La Motta, an ex-champ, considerably heavier than in his fighting days, is preparing for his dramatic reading before a cabaret audience. Always brilliant with filmic transitions, Scorsese cuts from La Motta's dressing room singing of "That's Entertainment" to a view of one of La Motta's 1941 fights, during which he gets hit in the face by his opponent. Surely this is entertainment to some, brutal though it may be; this crass attitude towards pain prepares us for the brutal coarseness that La Motta exhibits throughout the film. Yet *Raging Bull* turns this brutality to its

67

own benefit; Michael Chapman's brilliant cinematography pushes us right up against the fighters (and into the midst of La Motta's domestic battles), exposing all of the pain that is so much a part of this man's existence.

As a boxer and human being, Jake La Motta is predominantly bestial. It is no coincidence that his sport nickname is "the raging bull" (despite the amount of punishment he received, La Motta was never knocked down during the entirety of his professional career). Moreover, people throughout the film repeatedly refer to Jake as "an animal." Animal-like as well is the manner in which Jake's masculinity is strongly involved with demonstrations of his strength and endurance. At one point, La Motta laments the fact that he has "small hands," which he significantly calls "little girl hands." Immediately after this speech, when he asks his brother Joey (Joe Pesci) to hit him in the face, he accuses Joey of being "a faggot" when the punches don't bother him. Similarly, when Jake is scheduled to fight an opponent whom he considers a pretty boy, he characteristically comments, "I don't know whether to fuck him or fight him."

Jake's obsessive equation of male prowess with sexuality, and his inability to define his personality in anything other than the grossest physical terms, is traditionally animalistic, especially when we consider that in the animal world it is only the healthy, strong beasts—the ones that seem the most capable of enduring—that usually engage successfully in mating. In fact, the courtship rites practiced by many male animals involve demonstrations of their size and strength. These facts help to explain why Jake, in the only culminated (albeit off-screen) sexual encounter we are given in the film, initially shows Vickie (Cathy Moriarty) a picture of himself and his younger (and smaller) brother striking boxing poses, as though to prove his superiority, strength, and virility. Immediately afterwards, he has intercourse with Vickie for the first time.

Like many athletes, Jake subscribes to the belief that there is an antithesis between having sex and being at one's prime for a physical encounter with an adversary. Consequently, he refuses sexual contact with Vickie at one point because, as he says, "I gotta fight Robinson; I can't fool around." The implication here is two-fold: first, sexual satisfaction with Vickie is delayed in favor of the satisfaction that arises from his encounter with Robinson (sex is replaced by boxing, which must somehow be equally satisfying); second, unlike fighting, sex is not serious business; it is only "fooling around."

If we are to judge by the striking correspondence between his actions in and out of the ring, it is only through brutal physical encounters that Jake can express himself. While it is easy to see that he is truly in love with Vickie and his brother, he nevertheless finds it impossible to communicate with either (with the rare exception of the clowning he exhibits in his home movies) except through violence. Constantly obsessed with what Vickie's sexual activities are ("Did you fuck my brother; are you fucking him?") but unable to maintain a satisfactory sexual relationship with her (it is suggested more than once in the film that even when he's not preparing for a fight Jake hardly ever sleeps with his wife), he can only relate (in his own way) to Vickie and Joey (just as he had, apparently, with his first wife, Irma) by attempting to strike and maim them.

Love may in one sense be regarded as a transcendent experience sometimes expressed physically; such a view precisely corresponds to the manner in which La Motta interacts with his only formidable opponent, Sugar Ray Robinson. In the brutal fight during which La Motta loses the middleweight title back to Robinson, one can see in La Motta's insistence on taking more and more punishment from Robinson—and the manner in which he waits, only half-conscious, expectantly, for the *coup de grace*—intimations of a love/hate relationship being played out. Certainly, in La Motta's insistence that Robinson "never got me down" we hear the trumpeting of one's accomplishments before a revered enemy, and the unexpressed request for some form of acknowledgment from a person whom one respects. In many senses, the film depicts Robinson as La Motta's only truly complete lover.

Regardless of La Motta's pathetic plight—his loss of the title, his weight gain (turning him, as Pauline Kael said of the La Motta character's appearance late in the film, into "a swollen puppet"),[2] the break-up of his marriage, and his unfortunate conviction on a morals charge—*Raging Bull* nevertheless makes it difficult to sympathize with La Motta. Here is a man who beats his wife, almost as part of a daily routine; a man who constantly badgers his brother; a man who seems to have no friends.

After the loss to Sugar Ray and his rejection by Joey, Jake allows his only remaining valued possession—his tremendously resilient fighter's body—to fall apart. As he goes to fat, his attitudes about himself go to fat as well. His self-conception and personal habits become more and more degraded until, overweight and pitiful, he sinks to the level of a buffoon, becoming a third-rate stand-up comic and master of ceremonies in barroom dives. Even the routines we see him performing in his own club involve a kind of self-humiliation that is painful to watch.

The turning point for La Motta presumably comes when he is thrown in jail on a morals charge. Housed in a dark and squalid cell, now completely out of the public limelight (be it the spotlights in the ring or the ones in the club), he sinks into the cell's screen-right darkness and, resorting to the only means with which he is familiar, the physical, pounds his head on the wall in a futile act of penance, all the while screaming, "Why, why?"

It is after this flashback scene that we revert to the film's present tense, to La Motta rehearsing his act of readings from the works of writers such as Paddy Chayefsky (*Marty*), Rod Serling (*Requiem for a Heavyweight*), Shakespeare, Budd Schulberg (*On the Waterfront*, *The Harder They Fall*), and Tennessee Williams. The juxtaposition of these two scenes—the one leaving us with an image of La Motta frustrated over his stupidity (an underage female was served liquor in his club), the other showing us La Motta now decked out in a tuxedo—seems to imply that somehow Jake has achieved peace by attaining a proper perspective on himself.

The speech that he rehearses in front of his dressing room mirror—the "I coulda been a contender" piece from *On the Waterfront*—might, if taken at face value, suggest that even in defeat (like Terry Malloy at the appropriate point in the Kazan film), the speaker nevertheless retains a significant amount of dignity. The view that we are supposed to have of La Motta as a self-conscious, enlightened man (as the thoughtful Terry Malloy seems to be throughout the Kazan film) is reinforced by *Raging Bull*'s two closing titles, one a quote from John 9:24-26 (about the man who "once was blind but now . . . can see"), the other a dedication to Haig Manoogian, a co-worker (on *Knocking*) and NYU film teacher who presumably exerted a profound, positive influence on Scorsese.

The problem with *Raging Bull*'s end, though, is that there is no justifiable reason to assume that La Motta at this point is any different from the blind, egotistical oddity he has been throughout the film. Well-dressed in his tuxedo, he may be delivering passages on the fight game, but these stylized speeches about fighters' tragedies do not bear any necessary correspondence to La Motta's case. In fact, given the halting and unfeeling manner in which La Motta delivers the *On the*

Waterfront speech, one might be led to believe that despite the film's end quotation and epigraph, and despite La Motta's change in garb (which, in the vernacular, would be referred to as "a monkey suit"), La Motta is still predominantly "an animal," no different from the person we have known all along.

This is undoubtedly a problematic situation for the viewer: what are we to make of the film's sincerely offered ending quotation and dedication? I believe that we may recover the majority of *Raging Bull*'s effect and still not fault Scorsese for the ending's being inconsistent in tone with the rest of the production if we view the quotation and dedication as no more than Scorsese's observations on La Motta's life, with no implication that we are necessarily compelled to view them as strictly apposite to the film's events. After all, it is ultimately up to the viewer to determine whether or not these citations have relevance. We can reject their referential status and still be affected by the sincerity of the quotations, since even if La Motta is unchanged, the film—in attempting to find some core of meaning (realized or not) in Jake's life—may nevertheless be viewed as the instructive story of a pitiful man who deserves at the very least some of our sympathy.

Relying on the power of Robert De Niro's performance[3] to make La Motta in many senses a fascinating creature despite his human shortcomings, Scorsese manages to evoke an appreciable degree of, if not sympathy, at least non-judgmental interest. The successful creation of such an engaged attitude would itself be sufficient to rescue La Motta (in spite of his many brutalities) from condemnation, and thereby make of the film the story of a man condemned to fall short of success and exist in a moral and spiritual limbo—neither saved nor damned, pitifully poised on the brink of self-awareness without the sensitivity or intelligence to pass over into enlightenment.

NOTES

1.   That this didactic subtext is clearly Scorsese's intention is further affirmed by a statement the director made during the film's editing. Scorsese said that he saw La Motta's life as the story "of a guy attaining something and losing everything, and then redeeming himself." (Thomas Wiener, "Martin Scorsese Fights Back," *American Film*, November, 1980; p. 31.)

2.   *The New Yorker*, December 8, 1980, p. 217.

3.   De Niro won the Academy Award as Best Actor for his role in the film.

Chapter Eight

NO LAUGHING MATTER

The King of Comedy (1983) is not a comedy. This idiosyncratic, challenging film finds Scorsese returning seven years later to the
same basic themes and plot of *Taxi Driver*, with the difference that the
character Travis Bickle jestingly offered as his persona to one of the
Secret Service agents guarding Charles Palantine[1] has now become an
awkward and embarrassing reality, a man who only superficially seems
to be a fool.

The King of Comedy's premise and plot are quite simple. We
meet aspiring comic Rupert Pupkin (Robert De Niro) and his female
friend Masha (Sandra Bernhard), both of whom idolize late-night talk
show host Jerry Langford (Jerry Lewis). Rupert attempts to hold
Langford to his promise to listen to one of his demo tapes; Masha tries
to set up a private meeting with Langford; both fail. To get what they
want, they kidnap Langford and tie him up,[2] with the result that Rupert
appears as the first guest on Langford's show (which that night is
hosted by Tony Randall) while Masha has a secluded rendezvous with
the comedian. When Masha frees Langford from his restraints, he
slaps her and escapes. Rupert is sent to jail to serve two years of a
six-year sentence. When he emerges, he writes a best-selling book
about his escapade, sells the movie rights to the story for a sum in
excess of a million dollars, and gets his own television show.

What we have here is clearly a reprise of *Taxi Driver*'s basic
plot and denouement. The frustrated social misfit employs violence as
a means of realizing his ends. Rather than suffering for his actions, he
is rewarded. Travis becomes a media hero; Rupert not only wins public acclaim, but garners a great deal of money as well.

Unlike *Taxi Driver*, though, *The King of Comedy* yields little
if any pleasure during viewing. Instead, what the filmgoer experiences
is dread, a mounting sense of anxiety about Rupert's activities, and a
pronounced feeling of embarrassment in reaction to the way that Rupert

72

forces himself on people as though he actually had a talent deserving recognition (when in fact, as his Langford show performance makes clear, he is a terrible comedian).

One of *The King of Comedy*'s most daring qualities is the manner in which it presents to us characters whose personalities remain rigid and fixed, whose lives seem to take place inside of some great show business void. We know nothing more about Rupert at the film's end than we do at its beginning, and the same may be said for everyone else in the production. Quite possibly, the explanation is that there is nothing more to be learned about these individuals. Everyone appears to be one-dimensional (Rupert's high school acquaintance, Rita—whom he drags along on one of his embarrassing excursions—may be an exception, but her character is never developed), precisely because there is nothing more to them than what we are allowed to see. Given *The King of Comedy*'s overriding concern with the depersonalizing and dehumanizing aspects of the entertainment business, the unavoidable conclusion is that people in show business (or those enamored of it) are basically shallow. In essence, the only thing that counts for the performers is how they are perceived by the public. Image is all-important; everything else is inconsequential.

Moreover, none of the film's show business characters, especially the ones who are already successful, is interested in seeking out and presenting new talent. This is a highly understandable attitude given the intensely competitive nature of the performing arts. Still, the illusion that entertainers are approachable and concerned with improving the quality of their field by encouraging inexperienced performers must be maintained. Again, appearance is more important than reality.

This point is obviously one that Rupert simply cannot appreciate. In one of his fantasied meetings with Langford, Rupert imagines the star telling him how great his material is and how much he admires it. Langford goes on to assure Rupert that he would never think of stealing the material, that he is only interested in Rupert's success. It is clear that this sentimental view of the way that "stars" operate could only be spawned by someone like Rupert, who is too naive to know the truth.

Rupert fails to realize that there is more than just the entertainment side to show business; as the term denotes, it is a business as well. As Langford points out to the unperceptive Rupert during their brief limousine ride together, in this business—as in all businesses—you must observe the rules. In this case, that means starting at the bottom and gradually, through hard work and luck, climbing to the top of one's field.   Rupert, though, continues to believe that he will be discovered and immediately acclaimed as "the comedy find of the year" and be crowned as "the new king of comedy" (words he writes into his introduction on the Langford show).

Rupert's hunger for the life that he thinks celebrities lead overlooks the true nature of the existence into which notoriety thrusts one. As essayed by Jerry Lewis (on whose on-stage personality, and that of Johnny Carson, the character seems to be based), Jerry Langford is a singularly unattractive person: haughty, presumptuous, and short-tempered. What makes Langford doubly unattractive is the job that he performs. The position of talk show host is in itself quite demeaning. After all, here is a man paid large sums of money to orchestrate meaningless conversations with people only interested in sitting around and discussing themselves and their accomplishments (e.g. the pseudonymous author who, under the guise of idealism, has written a successful best-seller about "the vanishing Siberian tiger," and who is glimpsed selfishly, and violently, clawing his way into the Langford show studio when it turns out he will not be featured on that night's show to talk about his essentially self-serving campaign).

When Langford is seen at his show's beginning, strutting on stage with the characteristic Lewis swagger (the upper body held unnaturally stiff, the arms swinging at the sides), all Scorsese lets us see of his work is Langford making fun of show announcer Ed Herlihy's apparent inattentiveness ("Did I wake you, Ed?"), a lack of attention that may very well be due to the show's rather boring nature.

Throughout the film, Langford is portrayed as a self-centered individual whose characteristic emotions are rage, annoyance, and peevishness. With the exception of the crowd scene towards the film's beginning (the crush of the throng causes him evident distress, although he would doubtless be disappointed if a crowd had not gathered for him), Langford never exhibits any sympathetic emotions. Langford lives alone in a penthouse apartment, his only company a ridiculous Pekinese, whose sullen face and pampered accoutrements reflect its owner's situation. The penthouse furnishings are restrained to the point of sterility (although the apartment does feature four television screens, evidence of Langford's obsession with media), as are the sparse trappings at his weekend home.

The irony of *The King of Comedy* is that Rupert (whose haircut and manner of dress are crude imitations of Langford's) aspires to Langford's situation. Nor does Scorsese let us forget what kind of emotional vacuum Rupert desires to enter. Rupert has constructed in his basement a mock-up of the Langford show set; he sits in the set's middle chair, flanked by life-size cardboard cut-outs of Langford and "guest" Liza Minnelli as companions. The dummy figures' two-dimensional lifelessness acts as a mocking reminder of these super-stars' natures. When Rupert sits between these figures, engages in characteristic show business patter ("Liza, I saw your show"; "Jerry, you crack me up"), and displays the overtly exaggerated, false sentimentality (kissing so profuse that it becomes meaningless) that we've come to associate with late-night talk shows, Rupert is indeed a pathetic figure, still corporeal and alive, in contrast to the cardboard figures, but already poised on the edge of a lifeless, two-dimensional fame.

   Later, when Rupert practices his act, he does so in front of a huge blow-up photo of a smiling studio audience. He gestures in front of them and tells them jokes (which we do not hear; our suspicions about the quality of Rupert's act are not answered until the film's end),[4] while the soundtrack resonates with the laughter that Rupert has taped from some of Langford's television shows. During the monologue, Scorsese has the camera dolly back down a silver-colored corridor further and further until, at a pronounced physical distance from Rupert's performance, we achieve a figurative distance as well, and hear the canned laughter ringing with a mockingly hollow sound.

   Significantly, this view of Rupert is attained from behind him. Instead of being given the audience's point of view, we get the vantage point of the technician or performer behind the scenes. This privi-leged, insider's view only confirms our initial impression that the vacuity we intuit in this sequence is an accurate indication of the reality of show business.

   Even when Scorsese provides us with the audience's point of view, we are no closer to an accurate assessment of what the general reaction to Rupert's performance might be, since although we do see Rupert on the Langford show, we are never given audience reaction shots. All we see is Rupert, and all we hear is the audience's laughter and applause, reactions that (judging by Rupert's essentially second-rate material) must undoubtedly have been responses to applause signs and off-camera prompters employed by the show. The fact that the audi-ence can be so easily manipulated in this way only further cheapens the far-from-stellar qualities of Rupert's television appearance.

If any further confirmation were needed of the markedly unpleasant aspects of the fame to which Rupert aspires, one need only point to the speech in which Langford, while a hostage, tells Rupert and Masha about his life. Langford does not mention the pleasures of fine food and clothing, comfortable surroundings, and freedom from want that the money derived from fame can bring. Instead, with his face set into a virtual death-mask rigor, he talks about all of the terrible aspects of being a celebrity.

> I'm just a human being, with all of the foibles, all of the traps, the show, the pressure, the groupies, the autograph hounds, the crew, the incompetents, those behind the scenes you think are your friends and you're not too sure if you're gonna be there tomorrow because of their incompetence. There are wonderful pressures that make every day a glowing, radiant day in your life. It's terrific.

Characteristically, the meaning of this speech, the only sincere and impassioned dialogue that the film gives Langford, is completely ignored by Rupert, who blithely proceeds with his plot to appear that night on the Langford show.

Langford's staff and associates hardly display any more humanity than their boss. In fact, *The King of Comedy* demonstrates that the higher one proceeds up the ladder of success in show business, the more unsympathetic and unattractive are the people whom one encounters. The degree of humane treatment that Rupert receives is in inverse proportion to the power that the person dealing with him wields. It is the Langford office receptionist, the person who can do the least about getting Rupert's demo tape played, who treats him with the most sympathy. Cathy (Shelley Hack), a Langford aide, while polite to Rupert in an officially acceptable way, acts so mostly as a matter of course; indeed, under the guise of such politeness, she dismisses Rupert from the office with a studied kindness that makes her rejection that much more pronounced and cool.

When the most responsible members of the Langford organization are finally seen, they are revealed as nothing more than materialistic opportunists. While Langford is still being held prisoner, these men are reduced to squabbling about who is going to sue whom. Even when the business of rescuing Langford is attended to, one is left in doubt as to whether the comedian's release is being secured for humanitarian reasons or simply because he is needed for the continuation of his financially successful show.

To play the most powerful member of the Langford organization (Langford's executive producer), Scorsese uses Fred De Cordova, a veteran television professional who directed Johnny Carson's *The Tonight Show*. De Cordova's actions may be quite correct (he *does* arrange to have Rupert appear on the show) but his appearance is not in general attractive. Scorsese repeatedly shoots De Cordova from the left side of his face, thereby drawing attention to a rather pronounced, unappealing blemish on his upper cheek that could easily have been obscured by makeup or a change in camera angle. It is difficult to avoid the conclusion that in this respect (as indeed throughout the whole film), Scorsese is intentionally accentuating the least palatable aspects of the show business milieu.

Like Langford, his replacement, Tony Randall, is seen performing at only one point. Like his predecessor, when Randall takes over as substitute host, he effects laughter by maliciously ridiculing someone standing off camera, in this case the person holding the cue cards from which Randall reads. This is a crude form of humor, the lowest kind of comedy. By contrast, one must at the very least respect and admire Rupert's approach to comedy; his material may not be very good, but at least he doesn't resort to cheap insults to garner laughs.

Despite Rupert's eventual fame and fortune, what *The King of Comedy* ultimately leaves us with is an immense sense of emptiness and waste. Rupert is last seen onstage during his own television show. More an oddity and freak than anything else, he is absurdly dressed (in even worse taste than during the rest of the film) in a terrible red jacket, caught naked and alone in the glare of two spotlights while an off-screen announcer's introduction is repeated over and over again (a repetition of the echoes heard during Rupert's basement performance), resounding absurdly in the lonely and abstracted place where, thanks to his new-won fame, he will be condemned to dwell.[5] Unbeknownst to Rupert, fame's visitation is more a cruel prank than a hoped-for blessing, bringing with it a meaningless form of recognition that will doubtless turn Rupert into the image of the emotional cripple whom he idolizes: Jerry Langford. By *The King of Comedy*'s end there is nothing to laugh about except morbidity; presiding over the film's ironic black humor is the ultimate comic king, the figure who saves the nastiest joke for last, the cosmic ruler of emptiness and waste. The real king of comedy is death.

NOTES

1.   Travis told the agent that his name was Henry Krinkle, obviously the silliest name he could devise at the time.

2.   The viewer should note that while the violence in *The King of Comedy* (all of which is perpetrated by people desiring fame) is restrained, there are nonetheless a number of characteristic Scorsese foreshadowings of ominous events to come. The crowd waiting for Langford at the film's beginning displays an enthusiasm that borders on mania. Most significant is the manner in which Scorsese photographs Langford's walk from the stage door through the crowd, and to his limousine. Shot in slow motion, with Langford moving towards his car while Rupert is seen advancing towards Langford, the sequence takes on the ominous overtones inherent in the often-replayed news film of Jack Ruby, in slow motion, advancing on Lee Harvey Oswald to shoot him. *Taxi Driver*, too, cites the Ruby-Oswald shooting in the scene in which Travis (stationed, like Rupert, in front of and to the left of his "victim") moves towards Palantine in an attempt to shoot him. It would appear that Scorsese modeled both the *Taxi Driver* and *King of Comedy* scenes on that famous newsreel image, relying on disquieting emotional suggestiveness to create in us an anticipation of the violence that, in later sequences, both films will display.

3.   Rupert and Masha's abduction of Langford is anti-climactic; we have already vicariously experienced most of the action's violence in its anticipation. Since we know that the gun Rupert and Masha hold on Langford is not loaded, our sense of anxiety is somewhat relieved, although Scorsese again increases the tension by using a filmic cross-reference to make us feel uneasy. After Rupert and Masha have decided that Langford needs to be bound in his chair, Rupert says, "Sorry, Jerry," and Scorsese cuts to an overhead God's eye shot that cites both the prelude to the second murder sequence in *Psycho* and the overhead shot in *Taxi Driver* after the final cataclysm.

4.   However, we do know what an unself-conscious person Rupert is, a quality that may account for his inability to evaluate his material. Scorsese underscores this aspect by having a man sit in back of Rupert when he takes Rita out to dinner. For an anxious minute and a half, the man—who can easily be seen by Rita—mocks all of Rupert's wildly exaggerated gestures.

5.   Rupert's dream has come true; as in his basement fantasy, he stands before an audience that (if we are to judge by their knee-jerk laughter to his poor jokes) is as inherently lifeless as the people in his basement mural.

Chapter Nine

DEEP IN THE NIGHT

The works that *After Hours* (1985) most immediately call to
mind are the book and film versions of Franz Kafka's *Der Prozes*,[1]
especially with regard to the title's English version, *The Trial*, which
in one sense denotes a test. In this respect, the entirety of *After Hours*
can be read as a series of adventures through which Paul (Griffin
Dunne) must pass in order to attain some sort of goal. Yet as we see,
at the film's end Paul returns to where he started, which suggests that
despite his set of adventures, he hasn't learned a thing.

In a way, *After Hours* seems like an anticipation of Scorsese's
work in *Life Lessons*; the film is a minor work, a small movie without
great aspirations. But it has some significant points to make about
compromised lives and a failure of will, and if it doesn't wish to
venture outside of its limited world, that's actually to the film's credit.
After Hours makes the most of its confines. Indeed, the film's bound-
aries seem to be those of its protagonist, whose most prominent quality
is his almost morbid lack of ambition.

At the film's beginning, Paul is seated in a large office at a
desk identical to that of everyone else. When the young man whom
he's training proposes the idea of a literary magazine to him, Paul
looks away and doesn't respond. He's elsewhere. Yet almost immediately, the camera work frustrates our anticipation (just as the young
man's desire to be heard is frustrated) because Scorsese's tracking
camera shot from Paul's vantage point never lets us see what Paul is
looking at. This intentional misuse of the point-of-view shot, a
violation of the usual compact between audience and filmmaker, sets us
up for the subsequent frustration of expectations that we get throughout
the film. Just as in Sam Peckinpah's *Bring Me the Head of Alfredo
Garcia*, what at first seem to be excessive and discontinuous actions are
not to be read at face value but rather as intentional ruptures of
continuity intended to dislocate us from our usual mode of perception

79

so that we can more clearly appreciate the pathology of the central character.

It's clear early on in *After Hours* that Paul lacks resourcefulness. More so than *King of Comedy*'s Rupert Pupkin, the previous Scorsese character who was a product of the prevailing social system, Paul has very little imagination. Despite his being able to avoid capture and destruction, he seems more like a character buffeted by events than influencing them, an annoying figure whom we dispassionately observe. (He only elicits our sympathy at one brief point: when he breaks down over the death of Marcy [Rosanna Arquette].) After the rebuff of the aspiring literateur and the view of Paul's sterile apartment, we next see Paul in a cafe reading Henry Miller's *Tropic of Cancer*, which he tells Marcy is his favorite book, the only one in his collection that he rereads. The choice of favorite book should be a cue to the unreal aspect of the romantic assignation that follows, since the element of fantasy in the Miller book is quite pronounced. However, whereas *Tropic* is skewed in favor of the male, *After Hours* is tipped in favor of females, who control its action.

Much like *The Trial*'s Joseph K, whose sexual desires act as a corollary for his moral and spiritual imbalance (recall the manner in which, even when he is talking to his landlady, Joseph suggestively thrusts his hand into a pile of socks), Paul cannot seem to avoid situations in which women confound him. There are only two possible explanations for this state of affairs: on a realistic level, we could read the film as a series of actions involving manipulative women. It's just as likely, though, that what Paul is going through are projections of his own neuroses regarding women, that he is, in essence, creating the dilemmas in which he finds himself. Thus, regard the way that during what is a *non-sequitur*-laden conversation with Marcy, Paul suddenly becomes extremely hostile towards her. Apparently, what they've been smoking (which Paul says isn't marijuana, although it certainly seems to have *some* effect on him) unleashes all of his pent-up anxiety about his own ill-grounded personality, anxiety that he can only relieve by attacking someone else, which in the film is always a woman. The rest of Paul's adventures follow the same course of escalating danger, ultimately depositing him back where he began, with the strong suggestion that his character remains unchanged.

What happens in the film is that Paul passes into the night, through the looking glass of normal behavior and into an after hours region (in which, as a cafe owner explains, "different rules apply") situated in the seamy Hell of New York (characterized, as in *Taxi Driver*, by red vapors and slicked-down streets). Having stepped outside the bounds of his rigid personality, Paul seems destined to encounter trouble. At one point, *After Hours* seems to be operating on a principle derived from a pun. Both Marcy and Paul claim to have been traumatized by burns (whether or not these claims are true seems impossible to determine; although Marcie goes out to fill a prescription for a burn salve, her body is unmarked save for the tattoo that in one of the film's dead-end linkages somehow reminds Paul of the figure at the end of the keychain belonging to the bartender who, it turns out, is Marcy's boyfriend). The film repeatedly "burns" Paul, placing him in one hot situation after another, until finally he becomes the prey of an angry mob that is searching the neighborhood for him.

All of the interlocking pieces of information in *After Hours* fail to advance us towards an explanation for the film's unusual situations. As *Vertigo*'s Scottie Ferguson says, "if only I could find the key." For Paul, though, there is no key because there is no clue outside of nightmares (in which a completely different kind of logic applies) to explain events. Orson Welles, who directed and scripted a film version of *The Trial*, said of Joseph K:

> He's . . . a little bureaucrat. I consider him guilty.
> He belongs to something which represents evil and
> which is a part of him at the same time . . . he
> belongs to a guilty society, he collaborates with it.[2]

The sense of guilt in *The Trial* derives from Joseph's view of women as sexual objects and his role as a petty robot. In Paul's case, the same variables apply. Paul's apparent harmlessness is actually nothing more than a reflection of his lack of identity, which in the horror world of *After Hours* is the greatest crime of all. That plaster of paris shell that Paul breaks out of at the film's end represents the ultimate irony; when he's trapped in the artist's basement, he's most like himself: unable to move, barely able to be heard, very much as he was at the film's beginning, stiff-postured and with the same beady eyes darting back and forth. The irony is that as *After Hours* comes full circle, Paul's breaking out of his (literal and figurative) shell does nothing except leave him where he began: in the same stilted world as at the film's beginning, which collapses back into its meaningless self. The joke isn't very funny but the cautionary note is there nonetheless:

work in the system and you're a plaster of paris dummy in a meaning-less world.

The implicating force in *After Hours* is sex. In fact, there's a virtually Edenic curse on sex in the film's world. By yielding to sexual impulses, Paul is thrust back into a primitive, dream-like, mythic universe in which everything is exaggerated and in which desire equals guilt of the most damning kind. When Paul wonders aloud why terrible things are happening to him, and Scorsese has the camera blandly look down on Paul in a God's eye shot, we see in the camera work the latest in the film's ironies: that there's no answer possible from God because the fault lies in Paul. In this sense, despite its nightmarish aspect, *After Hours* has a very strict and identifiable ethos: that each individual is responsible for his or her own behavior, and must be on constant guard against moral collapse.

Throughout the film Paul demonstrates that he's a weak individual who is incapable of making a decisive move. The only significant action that he takes is to journey from his apartment, where we see him virtually comatose watching TV, to the cafe where he meets Marcy, and this is an action that is never depicted. He's an equivocator, too, incapable (or unwilling) to offer definitive opinions. Thus, when Marcy's friend Greg calls her, and Marcy complains, "How did that little faggot find out I was staying here tonight? Probably wants to whine to me about his latest boyfriend," Paul replies, "Friends like that are hard to deal with sometimes." When Marcy contradicts the tenor of Paul's remark, all he can weakly say in reply is, "Well, that's what friends are for."

It's no good for Paul (as for Joseph K) to contend that he's not guilty. Even though one of the leather boys in the bar says that Marcy's suicide isn't Paul's fault, we know that in an important sense Paul *is* responsible, and that Kiki is right: he walked out on Marcy after initially pursuing her (much as Joseph K does, first with Frau Burstner, then with the maid at the lawyer's). This attraction/repulsion attitude towards women is more than an example of indecisiveness; it's also a sign of manipulative hostility, an assertion of power: the power to disappoint.

In *After Hours* Scorsese's technique, which relies heavily on coincidence, black humor, and irony, serves him well. The style is virtually the meaning: intentionally cold and slick. The film is all smoke and mirrors. As in *The Lady From Shanghai*, the use of illusion communicates the idea that much of what we're seeing is illusory, the result of projections from the mind of a pathological individual. Indeed, the only significant reality in *After Hours* exists inside the mind of its petty central character.

NOTES

1. In fact, at one point in the film Paul has a conversation with a bouncer outside of a bar that he wants to enter which virtually duplicates the dialogue between the book's Joseph K and the gatekeeper guarding the entrance to the law.

2. Interview with Orson Welles in Welles, *The Trial* (New York: Simon and Schuster, 1970), p. 9. Not only much of *After Hours'* action, but also its milieu (e.g., Paul's office, which virtually duplicates Joseph K's office in the Welles film) seems derived from Welles' film.

Chapter Ten

TWO MINIATURES

Scorsese has directed two short films, one for broadcast television and one for theatrical release. His episode "Mirror Mirror" for
the Steven Spielberg series *Amazing Stories* (1985) and his portion of
the three-part *New York Stories*, "Life Lessons" (1989), both feature a
character who is singularly unlikable and who either avoids, or is
incapable of, any kind of self-awareness.

"Mirror Mirror's" Jordan Manmouth (Sam Waterston) is a
writer of grisly horror stories *a la* Steven King. When we first see
him, he is smugly primping on the Dick Cavett show. After the show,
he watches himself on TV from inside the limousine that is taking him
home.

On the surface, Manmouth's dismissal of his driver at the end
of the journey seems friendly enough but is actually tinged with a fair
amount of patronization. "I don't need you any more tonight," he
says, and the driver, required by the rules of this socio-economic game
of imbalance to be deferential, obsequiously takes his leave. Aside
from this interaction, the only real characterizing piece of business
comes when Manmouth stumbles on a young man who's stationed himself outside his doorway. Although the young man states that he's read
all of Manmouth's books and owns all of their editions, Manmouth's
only response is one of annoyance: he suggests to the youth that he not
bother him at his home, although it's obvious that the young man
would never be able to see him anywhere else. When the youth
accidentally drops some manuscript pages as he's leaving, Manmouth
becomes outraged. "So you're a writer too!" he says, giving him the
grudging suggestion that he learn how to type.

The zombie that Manmouth sees only in mirrored surfaces,
and who seems threatening to kill him, is more than just a double of
one of the zombies seen during the Cavett show in a clip from a film
based on one of Manmouth's books; he's also quite obviously a blatant

example of the *doppelganger*. Manmouth's eventual mental breakdown and final transformation into this zombie, after which he commits suicide, makes it clear that this grotesque figure represents Manmouth's crude and manipulative true self, this despite his pathetic calls for help to his girlfriend (Helen Shaver), which are no gauge of his emotional forthrightness since at that point in the teleplay his character is desperate for some form of assistance.

The problem with this twenty minute episode is that it builds up no tension. Manmouth sees his double, his ugly other half, and then becomes him. It's not as though Manmouth weren't already ugly enough; moreover, the transformation of the character into his double (which acts as an ironic twist on Manmouth's bitter comment to his driver that it's not the dead but the live ones you have to watch out for: "agents, ex-wives, journalists") violates the precepts of the *doppelganger* genre, in which the double is either not seen or never merges with the first self. After all, the *doppelganger* is a conceptualization, not a literal representation (the only time that a double assumes actual physical reality is when it turns out to be no double at all). In this genre there is always a necessary tension between the perceptions of the central character and actions in the real world, and it's precisely this lack of tension (which, as is usual with Spielberg, comes from a misunder-standing or gross manipulation of the genres from which he borrows all of his work) that becomes the episode's undoing.

In "Life Lessons," though, Scorsese is working from a much more intelligent script. The film (Scorsese's portion of the feature-length *New York Stories*) is not so much a dramatic action as a character study; Lionel Dobie's (Nick Nolte) personality doesn't change or advance, and his protege, Paulette (Rosanna Arquette), is there mostly as a foil to Dobie.

Dobie is an abstract expressionist painter; the only times that he actually creates anything representational is when he paints the small faces that, trapped in a world of swirling brushstrokes, peer out of the tapestries of his canvases. The faces mirror the situation in which Paulette, who wants to leave Dobie, finds herself: surrounded, virtually overwhelmed by Dobie's work. She's having major troubles of her own, though, trying to establish herself as a painter at the same time as she has to deal with Dobie. Paulette's paintings, transparently the work of someone who, at least in her art, has very little to say, are represented by the one painting of hers that we see, which, in another reflection of the imbalance between her and Dobie, is dwarfed by the two-canvas project on which Dobie is working. The people in Paulette's painting seem pathetic, two thin figures moving off to the left, one either leading the other in a chase or the two frolicking, but in a rather constrained fashion. There's no sense of freedom in the painting, although this quality may very well be a result of her relationship with Dobie, who smothers her personality with his wooly-bear gruffness.

Although he protests that he loves Paulette and wants her to stay under any conditions, Dobie nonetheless makes it plain that despite the life lessons he promises to Paulette's successor (a vow he undoubtedly made to Paulette as well), he has no wisdom or knowledge to impart aside from the inadvertent lesson that he teaches: not to become involved or remain in relationships that are based on manipulation. It's only in his art that Dobie becomes himself. As he tells Paulette, painting's "not about talent, it's because you have no choice." At the times when Dobie is painting, Scorsese's technique comes into its own. The director cuts from Dobie to the canvas on which he's working and sweeps in on the painting, closely following the artist's brushstrokes and moves. We see the canvas grow from a sketched-in series of arches to a multi-leveled creation; and though Dobie's character remains as flat and one-dimensional as a Rothko painting, in an ironic demonstration of the distinction between life and art, his work calls up the many layers of a Pollack.

Yet this multi-textured aspect collapses at the end of "Life Lessons" after Paulette has virtually left Dobie and he's already scouting for her replacement, with whom we're sure he will go through the same ritual of alternating protests of affection with demonstrations of manipulation. The real unidimensionality and flatness in the film emanate from the personality of Lionel Dobie himself. Incognizant of everything except aesthetic matters, Dobie proves that outside of his art he's incapable of any relationship other than the kind in which he treats his lovers like blank canvases on which he unreflectively smears his gobs of color.

Chapter Eleven

SCRATCH SHOT

Technique seems to be virtually all that Scorsese has at his disposal in *The Color of Money* (1986), which updates the story of *The Hustler* 25 years later. Paul Newman's Fast Eddie Felson returns, although this time he's not as fast as he was before (indeed, until the film's end, we don't even see Eddie playing pool). But he's still fast with his mouth and with the hustle that characterized him in the earlier film. At *Color*'s beginning, Eddie is smooth talking to Helen Shaver about the way the liquor they're drinking tastes, a virtual monologue from which he is distracted only by the pool playing of Tom Cruise's Vince, to which Eddie is drawn as to some fatal magnet.

Although Eddie is now a liquor salesman who drives a new Cadillac, you can see that he's very dissatisfied with his life. The wise guy banter and smooth face have given way to a tired patter and a supposedly sophisticated mustache, but mostly what characterizes Eddie is the fact that he apparently hasn't learned much in the years since his defeat at the hands of Minnesota Fats. Indeed, for all of the talking that Eddie gives Vince about how the kid has to rein in his natural tendency to show off in order to work his way up to the big hustle, it's clear from the film's end that all along, Eddie has been bluffing. He's not any smarter; he's a cocky braggart whose patter is meant to mask his egotism, that's all.

The film has as many obstacles in its path to success as Vince does. Newman's acting is enervated; he's trying to give us a portrait of a man who's tired out, who can barely work up the enthusiasm to talk a good hustle, but the lack of energy seems to emanate less from the character than the actor. Perhaps what Scorsese should have tried to coax from Newman was a bit more spirit in the playing, so that we'd know that there was still some spark left to Eddie. Otherwise, where's the pleasure in watching a character who makes no progression and is almost uniformly unpleasant?

This criticism extends to Tom Cruise as well. The script calls for Cruise to play his usual character, a spoiled egotist, and he does so with predictable results. Unlike Newman, though, Cruise seems incapable of achieving a distance between himself and the character he's playing, with the result that we're doubly alienated while watching him on screen. Thus, the degree of distaste that Eddie feels in watching Vince showing off in the pool halls is mirrored in the audience's reaction. Like Eddie, early on we've had enough of this kid.

The Color of Money is a very unpleasant film to view; only some of this response has to do with the action that the film describes. The film's colors, muted to reflect the dark world of the pool hustler, seem to grate on you with their lack of tonality, as does the inappropriateness of the white shitkicker music playing in a black pool hall. Perhaps what's worse is the insistent stylistics that repeatedly intrude, a result of Scorsese's attempt to support the story line. One might admire the use of cinematographer Michael Ballhaus' moving camera, which swoops around the pool players as they're taking their shots, but what does it add to the interest, excitement, and tension of watching the pool games to jump cut a series of pool shots, or to have the camera assume the point of view of a moving cue ball?

When Eddie arrives in Atlantic City and, on his own, inspects the hall where the tournament is to take place, Scorsese lines up the shot so that the great, empty, canopied hall with its eerily green pool tables and almost confessional lighting (one light over each table) looks like a church, one to which the devotional Eddie has finally returned. Unfortunately, Scorsese compromises the effect by unnecessarily putting organ music on the soundtrack. One can see that Scorsese is trying to show us how there's a virtually religious conflict in Eddie between his desire to once again score and his diminishing physical abilities (for one thing, his eyes are going bad), but the tension here between the word and the flesh seems forced and artificial. There was a true excitement to *The Hustler* that simply isn't present in *The Color of Money*, and we can't explain away the film's limp tone by appealing to the fact that Scorsese is telling a story about a central character who's lifeless. One could still tell such a story in an interesting way.

From almost the opening moments of the film, it's obvious that despite Eddie's antipathy towards Vince, he's also energized by his relationship with him, just as Vince is, to a degree, educated by exposure to Eddie. However, the film's action makes it clear that unlike most teacher/disciple films, in this one the teacher becomes disenchanted with his pupil, not only finally rejecting him but actually attempting at the end to best him in a competition. *Color* also emphasizes that the teacher is a highly flawed individual, who at the film's end needs to satisfy some basic urge to overcome the physical debilities that are rapidly overtaking him. I'd like to say that the film offers some new twist on the teacher/disciple theme, but even this aspect is overwhelmed by *Color*'s distasteful air.

Certainly there's a significant amount of antagonism between Eddie and Vince, but it never seems particularly interesting. And while Scorsese may be trying to tell us that it's not conflict but a similarity of character that keeps Eddie and Vince together, this aspect of the film also seems somewhat trite. Moreover, the interaction between Newman and Cruise seems formulaic. They never strike sparks; they merely raise their voices. At the film's end, Eddie isn't just (in his own words) "back" as a contender; he's also back with a nasty edge to him that even in the original film he never demonstrated. Exposure to Vince has brought back all of Eddie's worst qualities. Yet if by the film's conclusion the character repulses us, this may be precisely the effect that Scorsese intended. Unfortunately, it's an effect that is insufficient to redeem this misguided production.

Chapter Twelve

DESERT MIRACLE

Scorsese had been wanting to film Nikos Kazantzakis's *The Last Temptation of Christ* for many years. What is surprising and rewarding about this 1988 film is how devotional and restrained it is, especially given the nature of the material, which might easily lend itself to either an epic treatment or one in which the story's more fantastical elements could overwhelm the humanism and humor inherent in the material. Thanks to the work of screenwriter Paul Schrader, *Last Temptation* turns out to be a film with an appeal that cuts across religious and doctrinaire grounds.

To account for the groundswell of protests against the film is very difficult since there's virtually nothing objectionable in *Last Temptation* unless one objects to the humanizing of Jesus, something in keeping with the tenor of the synoptic gospels, in which Jesus' resistance to assuming his ministry seems very understandable. Indeed, it's clear that Jesus was a very fallible figure, with doubts and a volatile anger that are demonstrated in the Scorsese film.

The triumph of *Last Temptation* is that it takes one of the great stories and tells it (for the most part) realistically. There is no inappropriate overlay of stylistics for their own sake. When Jesus is in the desert and having visions, with the voice of Magdalene speaking to him through a cobra or, later, when Satan appears in the guises of a lion and then, subsequently, as a pillar of fire, we're not put off by the technique because we know that what we're seeing depicted is the Nazarene's interior state. And if there's no announcement of the shift from a realistic to a fantastical mode of representation, isn't that nothing more than a corollary for the way that these visions must have appeared unannounced to Jesus himself? Even when Jesus is healing the lepers, and the lepers' rising up out of their holes is represented in stretch-printed motion (a complement to the earlier effect of Jesus advancing through the desert via quick dissolves), neither of these techniques distances us from the material; their fantastical nature seems to grow out of it naturally.

The central dilemma in *Last Temptation* emanates from Jesus' dual nature, what the film in a preliminary title refers to as the eternal conflict between body and spirit. It's clear that this conflict is an elementary aspect of many religions, which speak to and through the flesh but appeal to the soul. What makes this particular film noteworthy, though, is that it successfully dramatizes this situation. Partly as a result of the fear of offending one group or another, too many other religious films hold their central subjects in such awe and reverence that the best the audience can do is vainly try to enter into the tenor of the proceedings. The Christ in films such as *The Greatest Story Ever Told* and *Ben-Hur* passes through each film with a halo of adoration swirling around his head. Such films speak only to people already convinced of Jesus' divinity, so they accomplish nothing in the way of widening Jesus' appeal. Moreover, *Last Temptation* raises questions about the religious experience that are rarely dramatized in films. Jesus' status as both god and man has not only provided the basis for a great many philosophical inquiries (Kierkegaard's *Fear and Trembling* is the most prominent) but also highlights the central dilemma of Catholicism. Jesus' crucifixion would have much less meaning if the Nazarene were certain that he was going to be redeemed. It's precisely Jesus' uncertainty, the foundation of his agonies and temptations, that paradoxically makes the crucifixion story so glorious, since it shows us a man dying for a cause whose validity is not—indeed, cannot—be firmly established. Jesus' triumph derives from his sacrificing himself solely on the strength of his faith.

The one prophet referred to in *Last Temptation*, Isaiah, made the point that the Jews had fallen away from the underlying humanism of their religion and instead gravitated toward the baser, material things in life. We can see an extension of this attitude manifested through characters in *Last Temptation*, Pilate among them, who scoff at Jesus, asking to see a sign or a miracle to convince them of the Nazarene's divinity. Yet such a sign or miracle wouldn't really be convincing since these miracles and signs, themselves a function of Jesus' great love and piety, might very well be ascribed to nothing more than magic. It's not the raising of the dead, the healing of the sick, the changing of water into wine, or even the transubstantiation (which Scorsese shows us taking place at the Last Supper) that are the convincing hallmarks of Jesus' divine mission so much as his followers' belief in him. In essence, Jesus asks for the Kierkegaardian leap of faith, just as *Last Temptation* asks us to suspend our own doubts in order to work its magic.

What helps to make *Last Temptation* convincing is the film's structure, which adds elements to the Jesus story that give us precursors of things to come. At the film's beginning, Jesus is, ironically, a maker of crosses. In much the same manner as we'll see him act on the way to his own crucifixion, Jesus carries across his shoulders the main brace of one of the crosses he's made; meanwhile, people revile and stone him. Two things are suggested herein: the eventual elevation to spiritual significance of material events, and an intimation of things to come. Indeed, prophecy is an integral part of the universe that *Last Temptation* creates. In fact, judging by the repetitions in the film, past and future are inseparable, since to make a distinction between them posits a view of time that is human-based and therefore, in the face of the overwhelming events of God's universe (which occur beyond time), irrelevant.

As shown through the film, it is the reward of God's plan that one can usually only realize the spiritual through the material realm. What *Last Temptation* posits is that once one realizes the essential divinity in all material things—as Jesus does when, late in the film, he sifts sand and calls it his body—one transcends the material aspect of objects and sees deep into their true nature, which is divine. Such a view moves us past notions of the contradiction between the material and spiritual realms and into a region in which both are complementary and there is free passage between them. Even the film's setting enters into consideration here. Judea is a region in flux, but one in which the essential turmoil between Rome and the Jews, between materialism and spirituality, between the body and the soul, are resolved, reduced to nothing by the uncompromising bright light and heat of the desert.

In the film Satan repeatedly attempts to speak to Jesus, tempting him in the desert and actually succeeding in deceiving him during the protracted amount of interior time that fills the film's last twenty minutes, when in what must have been a fraction of a second Jesus imagines that he lives the life of an ordinary man, with a wife and children.[1] However, *Last Temptation* demonstrates that the devil *can* be defeated, but that God cannot. When Jesus wants to rid himself of the pain of God that rips through him, a character points out, "what if it's God [inside you]? You can't cast out God, can you?" The point is that God lives inside Jesus' body (and by extension everyone else's) as a presence that is so strongly linked with the essential nature of human beings that, unlike Satan, he can't be cast out. Perhaps this is one of the ideas that critics regarded as heretical, for surely *Last Temptation* takes as its thesis the idea that not only is God in everyone but that he can, by extension, be apprehended by everyone through a process of spiritual cleansing and concentration. However, the implication that such an apprehension can (indeed must) be accomplished by the individual alone, apart from what is shown in the film to be the obtuseness of the traditional, money-oriented church and the ignorance of the rabbinate, is not only justified by the gospels but is the basis of all of the world's great religions.   *Last Temptation*'s Jesus doesn't know everything at all times. He's fallible, subject to desire, confusion, to sudden outbursts of anger and abandonments of will. Yet in the end, as the film comes full circle, not only fulfilling all of its prophecies but actually, in that split second on the cross, showing us Jesus intuiting the future destruction of Jerusalem and the conversion of Saul of Tarsus, we see that Jesus is a greater visionary than he has heretofore appeared.

By casting strongly contemporary actors in the lead roles (Willem Dafoe as Jesus, Harvey Keitel as Judas, David Bowie as Pilate, Barbara Hershey as Mary Magdalene),[2] Scorsese causes the film to be lodged in a timeless region by virtue of temporal contradiction: we're watching events that took place 2000 years ago at the same time as we're constantly drawn to the present through our views of the actors. Aware of the artificiality inherent in this scheme, we sense that the characters have a dual substance that complements the film's main dilemma.

The film's most striking quality, though, is the change that it apparently effected in its director. For a brief period, in that barren location, Scorsese himself seems to have wandered off into the desert and, for a time, resolved all of his own doubts and anxieties. Through the vehicle of *Last Temptation*, director and audience come at last to some sort of crazy peace through paradox.

NOTES

1.   It may very well be this aspect of the film that proved to be most offensive to doctrinaire Christians.
2.   In particular, the use of Dafoe is noteworthy. Scorsese has taken advantage of Dafoe's sharply-defined features and turned them to

account.   The physical characteristics in Dafoe that seemed threatening in William Friedkin's *To Live and Die in L.A.*—his rough-hewn face and crooked smile—here come to reflect Jesus' inner torment and wry humor.   Dafoe's Jesus looks tortured and ascetic, precisely the appearance we'd expect in someone who has become the battleground for a fight between disbelief and devotion.

Chapter Thirteen

WISE GUYS

"Three generations of life in the Mafia," the way that *GoodFellas* (1990) was billed, is hardly adequate to describe the textural richness of this film. It's more than a story about a group of gangsters, the kind of story Scorsese has told before in *Mean Streets*. Nowhere else in the director's films is his concern with the Italian-American experience, the need for and demonstration of male bonding, the puckish sense of humor, and the utter command of technique (here subordinated, as it should be, to the film's thematic elements) so successful and so pronounced. With the carryover from *Taxi Driver* of voiceover narration providing a strong unity in the midst of what is often quite chaotic action, *GoodFellas* qualifies as Scorsese's contemporary masterpiece.

Although a portion of the film is narrated by someone else, *GoodFellas* is Henry Hill's (Ray Liotta) story, and Scorsese wastes no time in setting it up. In order to gain our attention from the outset, Scorsese begins the film with an excessive piece of action: the repeat stabbing and shooting of Billy Batts, whom Henry, Tommy (Joe Pesci), and Jimmy (Robert De Niro) have stuffed into the trunk of their car. It's in the red-tinged blast furnace light of the gun shot, this after Tommy has stabbed Billy, that the film's narration begins. Scorsese freeze-frames the shot on Henry, focussing our attention on him just as the narrative technique does, and then shifts us back in time to the younger Henry. What the director thus accomplishes is an immediate establishment of interest in the character. Although he then zooms us back in time to sketch in Henry's background, he's piqued our interest in the Billy Batts story so that we look forward to the narrative's eventually catching up to where it began. And though it takes an hour or so for this to happen, we really don't mind; *GoodFellas'* action is so diverting, and the performances of the film's principals are simultaneously so humorous and alienating, that the time passes quickly.

95

In his essay on the western, Robert Warshow noted the similarity between the Old West gunfighter and the gangster: both are men with guns.[1] Certainly in *GoodFellas* there is an almost morbid fascination with gunplay, not only on the part of the audience (the bloodletting is at once entrancing and alienating) but also on the part of the film's characters. *GoodFellas* not only dramatizes the gangster experience but demonstrates that its gangsters are not, as were their counterparts in films from the 30s, working in opposition to the law. If anything, they are complements to traditional policemen, who more than once in the film are seen operating in complicity with criminal activities.

It's clear that the gun opens up a world in which each man becomes his own law; and make no mistake about it, this is a world dominated by men (the only time that we see a woman handling a gun is when Henry's wife Karen [Lorraine Bracco] points one at him). However, the loneliness and melancholy that Warshow posits in the western hero and the gangster[2] are not, at least initially, predominant qualities in *GoodFellas*. As with *Mean Streets'* Giovanni and *The Godfather'*s Don Corleone, what at first characterizes the gangster in *GoodFellas* is his sense of community and need to belong. The young Henry Hill, staring out of his apartment window at Tuddy's cab stand (at that time the base for Paulie's [Paul Sorvino] empire), wants to be a part of the action. It's not a question of greed or ambition; he simply yearns for the identification that's made possible by membership in a social group. Alienated from his tumultuous and unhappy home life, he gravitates toward the locus of power that he intuits at the cab stand. "As far back as I could remember I always wanted to be a gangster," he says. For Henry at this point, being in the mob means money, women, power, and the ability to dress well, the latter point comically handled when Henry comes home wearing a mob-bought suit and his mother, aghast, says "You look like a gangster." In this nighttime-oriented world of killing, mayhem, and male bonding, appearances count for a lot: thus the way that Jimmy Conway flashes money the first time that we see him, stuffing twenty dollar bills into people's pockets (a gesture that Henry will virtually repeat when he takes Karen out to a nightclub). Scorsese uses a great deal of point-of-view shots in the film, which not only act as a corollary to the emphasis on appearances but also reinforce the bias of the single narrator technique.

"I was part of something; I belonged . . . I was living in a fantasy" Henry says. Yet after we've been inside the *GoodFellas* milieu for a while, it doesn't seem like a fantasy any more; it seems real, which is undoubtedly the way it appears to the film's characters, whose only frame of reference is their own world. Although the men like to buy things for themselves and their women, for the most part they don't seem to be living very lavishly. Karen observes that the women all have bad skin and dress in poor taste, but their men aren't really doing any better with their wing collars, flashy suits, and the appearances they make in tawdry nightclubs (the Copacabana sequence is the only exception here). The problem is, though, that these men have no self-consciousness, since they have no contact with an outside reality that would suggest to them the negative insularity of their lifestyle.

In *GoodFellas*, old country tradition continues in America. Paulie sits in his backyard at a barbecue and receives tribute from various people. He almost never talks to anyone directly, speaking instead through his brother as though he were an ancient potentate. With the camera set to slight slow motion, Scorsese photographs Paulie chewing on a sausage sandwich and just barely nodding a "yes" to a man who's in need of help (a labor dispute, a contentious person who needs to be killed? No problem). As Henry describes it, Paulie provided "protection for people who can't go to the cops . . . a police department for wise guys." It's not a positive quality, though. Usually, the only people who can't go to the police are those involved in some criminal activity. Yet the way Henry characterizes it, it's as though the gangsters are a bunch of Robin Hoods helping the righteous poor.

Just like the westerner, these men live by a code, one communicated to Henry after he gets arrested for the first time. "You've learned the two greatest things in life," Jimmy tells him. "Never rat on your friends and always keep your mouth shut." When Henry is greeted on leaving the courtroom (where, judging by the nod between the defense attorney and the judge, the fix is already in), Paulie says to him, "You broke your cherry," indicating that for these men breaking the law is an initiation rite. Yet we laugh at the statement. Only later in the film do we realize that the way these men live is terrible, mostly as a result of the actions of their most excessive member, Tommy.

GoodFellas defines the classic Joe Pesci character: fast talking, foul-mouthed, and homicidal, with a short-fused temper that easily explodes into unexpected violence, as when Tommy kills Billy Batts and, later, the innocent kid Spider, just because they insulted him.

"I'm just breaking your balls," Batts had told Tommy; and Spider, telling Tommy to "Go fuck [himself]" days after Tommy had shot the kid in the foot is just giving back (albeit in small measure) what he got. The point in both of these instances, though, is that Tommy loses face; and though Jimmy, after asking Tommy "You gonna let him [Spider] talk to you that way?" later says that he was only kidding in goading Tommy, the fact is that Tommy explodes because he feels that he's been insulted. For Tommy, the fact that his retribution takes the form of murder is inconsequential; what counts is responding at all.

Yet such an excessive response is no different in kind than the powerful presumptuousness that these men continually exhibit. "Saturday was for the wives but Friday was for girlfriends," Henry says, as though the world and human relationships could be that easily compartmentalized. And when the men talk about the Lufthansa heist, Henry justifies it by saying, "We grew up near the airport; it belonged to Paulie . . . whenever we needed money we'd rob the airport; it was better than Citibank." These men see no contradiction between their actions and any kind of independent law or morality, a consideration that brings up the question of the Catholic presence in the film.

There are only two literal religious references in *GoodFellas*, and they both involve women. When Henry first calls on Karen at her home, the crucifix that he wears around his neck is prominent. Karen covers it up because she's told her family that Henry is half Jewish. "Which half?" Karen's mother asks and Henry replies, "the good half." The remark makes it clear that religion is obscured in the film, that its usual behests to live a moral life have nothing to do with the way that these men live. Moreover, in his impromptu remark, Henry inadvertently reveals not that Judaism is better than Catholicism but that at least half of him is corrupted.

The second time that religion surfaces is when Tommy, on the way to "being made," asks his mother to not paint religious pictures, a remark that throws us back to an earlier scene. When Tommy stops at his mother's for a knife to stab Billy Batts, there's a juxtaposition of religion with violence that shouldn't go unnoticed. Tommy's mother displays a painting she's recently done of a man and two dogs in a boat. It's a rudimentary work, but what's significant about it is that the man in the boat looks like a patriarch and is situated in a placid, almost biblical scene. The religious connotation of the painting operates in violent contradiction to what's going on right outside Tommy's mother's kitchen window: Billy Batts struggling for his life in the trunk of the car (Scorsese zooms in on the trunk to emphasize the point). Religion and violence, then, not only go hand in hand; Scorsese is also suggesting that for these men, violence *is* a religion, a virtual sacrament of behavior.

But then what counts isn't the underlying religious reality but the way that things look, as Paulie tells Henry after Henry has been spending a lot of time at his mistress' apartment. It's a sentiment echoed by Jimmy when he tells Henry, "You have to do the right thing; you have to go home to the family," and Paulie continues, "You're not gonna get a divorce; we're not animals." Intriguingly, Jimmy and Paulie define the "right thing" as going home to a family that doesn't really constitute a family (Henry has been cheating on his wife for years, even allowing his mistress to visit him while he's in prison). Does it make Henry less of an animal because he remains in a faithless relationship? That's what these men apparently believe, and here we can see their utter hypocrisy and self-serving attitudes. Despite their talk about good fellows and friendship, what counts for these men is getting what they want and screwing everybody else. Thus, towards the film's end, when things start to fall apart, the men begin to turn on one another. It's here that the qualities of aloofness and alienation that Warshow describes begin to emerge.

> . . .the gangster's loneliness and melancholy are not "authentic"; like everything else that belongs to him, they are not honestly come by: he is lonely and melancholy not because life ultimately demands such feelings but because he has put himself in a position where everybody wants to kill him and eventually somebody will. He is wide open and defenseless, incomplete because unable to accept any limits or come to terms with his own nature, fearful, loveless. And the story of his career is a nightmare inversion of the values of ambition and opportunity.[3]

Dramatizing these qualities, there's a fascinating sequence in which Karen visits Jimmy after Henry has been arrested and it seems as though Jimmy, who has always seemed to be the most private and introspective (and thereby the most dangerous) of all the men, is setting her up to be killed. When Jimmy directs her towards an alley where there are supposedly some designer dresses but in which all that we see are two men lurking in the shadows, we get the feeling that the whole scene's jittery aspect reflects either Karen's paranoia or a strangeness in Jimmy's behavior. It looks as though the latter is the case, especially considering the way that Jimmy later suggests that Henry go down to Florida to do a job for him and it appears that Jimmy is merely setting Henry up to be killed (probably so that he won't inform on Jimmy, which he nevertheless does). At this point, fraternal bonds are disintegrating. Jimmy is responsible for the deaths of many people involved in the Lufthansa heist, Maurie and Vinnie among them. These actions prepare us for Henry's breaking the code of silence when he makes a deal with federal agents to turn informant in exchange for protection.

Having been initiated into the mob through blood (predominantly through the first shooting that he sees, when a man who's been shot falls down outside Paulie's pizzeria and Henry mops up some of the blood with an apron; Karen had been similarly initiated when Henry has her hide a blood-stained gun), Henry nonetheless turns against his friends when it becomes an issue of saving himself, a fact that gives the lie to all of the buddy-buddy talk throughout the film. ·

Towards *GoodFellas'* end, Scorsese speeds up the action with rapid cutting and action, all reflections of Henry's frenzied state, the result of his dealing and snorting cocaine. By the time he turns state's evidence and informs on Jimmy and Paulie, Henry's identity—the only one he's ever had—has disappeared, a change in the film cued by Henry's stepping down off the witness stand, walking out of the narrative mode, and addressing the camera directly, something that has never before happened. As he says at this point, "My birth certificate and my arrest sheet; that's all you'd ever have to know I was alive," a statement which means that between being born and the present in which he's speaking, Henry hasn't really accomplished anything at all. He's been a cipher. Henry remarks at this point that he's being compelled to leave "the life." The usage is significant because the phrase usually refers to prostitution. Henry has prostituted his entire existence through an association with men whose devotion (with the possible weak exception of Paulie) means nothing at all: when it profits them to do so, they abandon each other. Finally, after he has entered the witness protection program, Henry is even unable to get a proper mob-associated meal. "Right after I got here I ordered some spaghetti and marinara sauce. I got egg noodles and ketchup." It's a wise guy exit line, suggesting along with his subsequent statement (that now he's

"an average nobody . . . get to live the rest of my life like a schnook")
that he still misses the corrupt values of the mob that never really did
a thing for him, an indication of the character's essential blindness and
stupidity that is the strongest condemnation of mob life Scorsese is ever
likely to give us.

NOTES

1.   Robert Warshow, *The Immediate Experience* (New York: Atheneum,
        1979), p. 135.
2.   Ibid, pp. 136-137.
3.   Ibid.

Chapter Fourteen

THE TERROR COAST

One can see from the outset what Scorsese intended with his remake of *Cape Fear* (1991): he's showing us a world that in the 29 years since the original film has, in moral terms, turned upside down. In the film's view, one can no longer rely upon the traditional values of right and wrong to help one identify what one should and should not do. However, in an obvious attempt to modernize what Scorsese apparently felt was a creditable plot structure, the director has muddied the original film's ethical waters, transforming Max Cady (Robert De Niro) from a guilty character into a man who has a justifiable grievance against lawyer Sam Bowden (Nick Nolte).

Bowden's family has been differently conceived as well. In this often contentious family, in which the lines of authority and respect have broken down, the mother and father are at odds with one another over Bowden's past (and possibly present) infidelity. The daughter, who in the original film exhibited a striking sexual precociousness, has that precociousness updated to a contemporary form. Thus, where the original film's Cady commented on Danielle's being cute, in Scorsese's version Cady not only encourages Danielle's sexuality by giving her a Henry Miller book but, in the film's most effective scene, actually gets her to suck his fingers in an action that is strongly suggestive of fellatio.

In Scorsese's film, both Danielle (Juliette Lewis) and Bowden's wife Leigh (Jessica Lange) are sexually threatened by Robert De Niro's Cady. The fact that the family's protection figure and father is morally compromised opens the way for Cady's assault against their home which, like the farm attack in *Straw Dogs*, tends to become an analogue for an assault against the body. Yet despite the ultimate resolution of the assault, it's still clear that in both versions of *Cape Fear*, the threat of Cady's sexual aggression derives from his outrage over what he considers the unjustness of his conviction. While the

102

latter aspect is certainly strongly present in Scorsese's version, it is eclipsed by the leering expressions of Robert Mitchum in the original film, who from the very beginning is ogling women. Yet in both versions Cady early on makes it clear that his primary method of revenge will be to violate the sanctity of Bowden's home life. In this sense, the Scorsese film makes Cady out to be less of a threat than he might otherwise be, since Bowden's family milieu is already significantly sullied. Nonetheless, there are other striking differences between the film's two versions that bring the qualities of Scorsese's film into relief.

For one thing, in the original film Bowden didn't withhold evidence that would have aided Cady's case. And though the law in both versions is equally powerless to stop Cady, with the police chief in the earlier film commenting, "Either we have too many laws or not enough," the appearance in the earlier film of Gregory Peck as Sam Bowden goes a long way towards defining the variations between the two versions. Peck's moral rectitude (a quality that he would also most successfully project in 1962's *To Kill a Mockingbird*) is only discredited when he hires thugs to assault Cady (an act which, if we can't forgive, we can at least understand). In the later film, Nick Nolte brings to the role a contemporary attitude that is not only more accepting of moral compromise but is even capable of it. The distinction between the two Sam Bowdens carries over to his wife, with the original version's Mrs. Bowden (Polly Bergen) always exuding primness while in Scorsese's film, Leigh Bowden is far more progressive and compromised, demonstrating in an early scene a degree of alienation between herself and her daughter that would have been conceptually impossible in the earlier film.

While Nancy/Danielle remains provocative in both films, the real distinction between the films lies in the character of Cady himself. Although both Cadys have obviously studied the law, Robert De Niro's Cady is not only more intelligent than Mitchum's but, in an analogue to his mania for revenge, has his fierceness magnified by his religious obsession. Given Cady's religious bent and the way that in Scorsese's film it sets him apart from his predecessor, it is therefore ironic that in Scorsese's version Cady is more justified in seeking revenge, since Bowden withheld evidence that would have aided his client's case, a fact that grants Cady a degree of moral rectitude that seems out of place in a film in which everyone is guilty of some kind of moral lapse.

fact that grants Cady a degree of moral rectitude that seems out of place in a film in which everyone is guilty of some kind of moral lapse.

Indeed, given this schema, it almost seems as though Cady is the only one of the central players who is a candidate for the audience's sympathy. While such an approach to characterization is in keeping with *Cape Fear*'s intentionally corrupt morality, it also places the audience in an extremely difficult position. How can we approve of Cady given his homicidal abuses? Scorsese seems to have made a conceptual mistake (one that he also committed in *The Color of Money*): he has appropriated contemporary cynical values only because they seemed to be convenient for his film. As might be expected, the result is unconvincing.

Complementing the manner in which Scorsese's film shows us a universe that is ethically inverted (at one point, on the phone with Danielle, Cady hangs upside down while he pretends to be her new drama teacher), actors from the earlier film appear in roles that modify their moral status. Mitchum appears as a policeman, but one who recommends to Bowden that he take the law into his own hands (precise-ly what Mitchum's Cady does in the earlier film); Martin Balsam appears as a judge who, unlike his police chief from the earlier film, would never accede to the kind of entrapment that his character in the earlier film recommends; Peck himself resurfaces in the role of a lawyer, with the expected twist that this time, he's representing Cady.

The difference between the two films is most strikingly evident in their school pursuit sequences. Although in both films the initial meeting between Nancy/Danielle and Cady takes place in a school, in the earlier film the little girl is portrayed as an innocent victim of stalking, cringing in the school locker room as a man whom she believes to be Cady comes walking toward her. In Scorsese's film, though, Danielle actually meets Cady, in the school theater, usually a place of illusion and trickery, where Cady brings home to her a powerful lesson in reality. Cady sits in grandma's house from *Little Red Riding Hood*, simultaneously assaying the part of the wolf and the innocent. When he steps out of the house and lowers Danielle's inhibitions with a few drags from a marijuana cigarette, we find that, unlike Nancy in the first film, Danielle is fascinated by Cady's gross animality (just as the woman whom Mitchum picked up in the earlier film had been). Danielle's complicity in this scene, taken along with the characteristics of her parents that I've already pointed out, makes it seem that Cady's movements against the family do indeed have an element of Old Testament justice about them.

The family's dysfunctional aspects make it clear that there's very little, if any, affection among these people, so that where in the earlier film Cady's threats seemed deplorable not only because they were shocking but also because they markedly contrasted with the Bowdens' peaceful family life, in the present film, Cady's antagonistic behavior makes him seem so similar to the Bowdens that he might just as well be a member of the family.

What we're really seeing dramatized through Cady's actions in Scorsese's *Cape Fear* is the Bowdens getting what they deserve. We can see the family's guilt concretized in the manner in which Scorsese sets up the film's last scene. Where in the earlier film the houseboat, a symbol of the Bowdens' innocent, beleaguered status, is used only as bait to entice Cady towards a place where the family seems isolated, in Scorsese's film it is suggested that the boat represents a concretization of the family's being morally adrift on what are increasingly perilous waters. As a result, the storm that comes down on the Bowdens in Scorsese's film isn't just a natural phenomenon; it's also a symbol of judgment against them.

Yet Cady's presumptuous aspect also enters into play here. His self-appointment as judge and jury is more than a reflection of the manner in which Bowden, by withholding evidence, took on these roles, since Cady exceeds Bowden's act by also assuming the role of execu-tioner. And though the houseboat sequence runs on too long, and includes elements that tax credibility (in particular Cady's repeated returns from the dead so that he begins to resemble *Halloween*'s Michael Myers or *Friday the Thirteenth*'s Jason), throughout the sequence Scorsese is in dramatic control of the proceedings, although even this quality disappears when he uses split diopters—showing two characters in different planes in sharp focus as an analogue of group complicity—or negative images. But the main failing of Scorsese's film is that it seems to have updated the material mostly to satisfy an intellectual conceit on the part of the director. Scorsese's *Cape Fear* gives us no added insight into the characters, just an opportunity to see what Robert De Niro would do in the role of Cady, an aspect that fails to come off very successfully since De Niro seems constantly to be playing against type: he's too cerebral an actor to do a Robert Mitchum imitation.

In *Cape Fear* Scorsese makes a pitch for acceptance by the mass audience; this is clear from the film's extremely polished production design and, perhaps most notably, its violence, which is far more graphic than in the original. However, unlike the violence in Scorsese films such as *Taxi Driver* or *GoodFellas*, *Cape Fear*'s violence (as in the assault against the woman whom Cady picks up in a bar) seems excessive and gratuitous. Scorsese would have done better to have remained on familiar territory and scouted out the intelligent conceptual landscape that in previous films he has demonstrated he knows so well.

Chapter Fifteen

TASTEFUL RESTRAINT

From the beginning moments of *The Age of Innocence* (1992), with Saul and Elaine Bass' title sequence showing flowers slowly opening, the images gracefully dissolving into one another, we know that there is a style and fluidity to the film that promises much that is new. And while at first one might have surmised that the film, a period piece about a disappointed romance, does not seem typical fare for Scorsese, the plot of the film does, in fact, fit perfectly within the director's *oeuvre*.

One can imagine what attracted Scorsese to the project. Edith Wharton's story, as it is reconceived by Jay Cocks and the director, presents us with an almost classical conflict in Newland Archer (Daniel Day-Lewis) between the social mores that prescribe behavior and his innermost impulses, which incline him towards a love affair with the Countess Ellen Olenska (Michelle Pfeiffer), although Archer's ingrained sense of propriety compels him to remain engaged to May Welland (Winona Ryder), who at first glance appears oblivious to her fiance's true thoughts and feelings. To view the story in such a way, though, is to react only to its surface—and yet surfaces are a great deal of what the film is about: the light from candelabra glinting off of silverware, reflected in the glasses of old men, bounding off the elegantly prepared foods over which Michael Ballhaus' camera lingers. It is precisely in its allegiance to the surface of things, to appearances as they are manifested in the realm of acceptable behavior as opposed to the integrity and reality of emotions that are nonetheless buried, that the conflict in the film occurs. Swirling around as slowly as the smoke from the cigars of men in drawing rooms after dinner, though, are the eddies of emotional dissatisfaction that inform Archer's nature, which silently rebels against being compelled to behave in "acceptable" ways.

What the ambiguity of the film and book titles accomplishes is a collapsing of two realms, the historical and the personal. The repression of emotion displayed by Newland reflects an identical repression on the part of the nation as a whole, with a similarly bleak auguring for the future in both realms.

There is a discrepancy in the New York society between what men are allowed to do and what is deemed proper for women; yet the men's behavior, at least if we are to judge it by Newland's, is restricted as well. In the book, Archer's uncharacteristic condemnation of Beaufort, who in both film and novel is the only character who behaves without regard for what people think, indicates that in a significant way Newland envies Beaufort's audacious freedom, which Archer cannot hope to attain without exercising an act of will of which he is simply incapable. Indeed, the unnatural split in Archer between his conscious actions and his impulses makes it plain that he is unable to face the contradiction in his behavior; he merely acts without reacting to the significance of his acts.

Scorsese reportedly worked on the gastronomical aspect of the film for over two years, researching the various kinds of foods that the characters would have served. We can appreciate the film's obsession with detail as a reflection of the 1850 society's concern with appearances; yet the film's fixation on foods and furnishings seems smothering and overpowering. In previous films (e.g., *Boxcar Bertha*, *New York, New York*, and the early parts of *GoodFellas*), Scorsese has shown us just how accurately he can portray a certain time or place. Surely, though, what should be of paramount importance in any film is the inner logic of its characters' actions, not the verisimilitude of the trappings against which this action takes place.

One of the film's interesting qualities is that it inverts Scorsese's usual emphasis. Generally, Scorsese is concerned with psychological activity as an adjunct to forms of excessive behavior; it is only through the exaggerated actions of his characters that we intuit what it must be like for them to be who they are. In *The Age of Innocence*, though, the psychology of the characters is not only couched but is melded with actions that themselves reek of repression.

Scorsese has been widely praised for his work in *Age*, especially with regard to transcending his genre filmmaking and branching out in a new direction. I want to be fair to Scorsese, but merely venturing into new territory is not in itself a virtue, especially if one is not particularly suited to it. There is an enervated feel to this film that simply is not present in most of Scorsese's other work. Perhaps in remaining true to his source material, Scorsese has committed a grave error; the film is tasteful, but it is also drawn out and not particularly memorable.

It's clear that Scorsese wanted to have a commercial hit on his hands and, at least in terms of grosses and publicity, *The Age of Innocence* qualifies in this respect, a situation that the admirer of Scorsese's work should find gratifying. At the same time, though, one cannot help but regret the subordination of the director's usual obsessions in the service of what is essentially a closet drama. Regardless of its effect on you, it could never be said of any previous Scorsese film that it didn't in some manner leave you with a strong impression (this is true even with regard to *The Color of Money*, in which Scorsese's concerns can be intuited bubbling under the film's surface). But do we really leave *The Age of Innocence* with anything other than an appreciation for the beauty of its realization as opposed to the dynamic and insightful way that it might have probed under its characters' actions for the powerful psychological forces that have always been a hallmark of the director's filmmaking? It may, perhaps, be precisely by virtue of its cultured facade that *The Age of Innocence* has subverted itself.

The film is beautifully photographed and admirably restrained; but restraint for some directors may herald somnolence of their best artistic instincts. *Age* is more a feast for art directors, production designers, and food connoisseurs than anything else, and even some of its kindest critics have been careful to point out that the subterranean aspect of the film's emotions seems to work against it. Such tastefulness is purchased at a fairly high price, in this case the fascinating energy that Scorsese's best films always evidence.

WHO'S THAT KNOCKING AT MY DOOR (1969)

Direction: Martin Scorsese
Script: Martin Scorsese (with additional dialogue by Betzi Manoogian)
Cinematography: Michael Wadleigh, Richard Coll, Max Fisher
Editing: Thelma Schoonmaker
Sound: John Binder, Jim Datri
Art Direction: Victor Magnotta
Producers: Joseph Weil, Haig Manoogian, Betzi Manoogian
Distributor: Joseph Brenner Associates

Cast: Harvey Keitel (J.R.), Zina Bethune (The Girl), Lennard Kuras (Joey), Michael Scala (Sally Gaga), Anne Collette (young girl in dream), Harry Northup (Harry, the rapist), Robert Uricola (young man at party with gun), Bill Minkin (Iggy/radio announcer), Wendy Russell (Gaga's girlfriend), Phil Carlson (the guide on the mountain), Susan Wood (Susan), Marissa Joffrey (Rosie), Catherine Scorsese (J.R.'s mother), Tsuai Yu-Lan, Saskia Holleman, Ann Marieka (dream girls), Victor Magnotta, Paul de Blonde (boys in street fight), Martin Scorsese (gangster), Thomas Aiello.

BOXCAR BERTHA (1972)

Direction: Martin Scorsese
Script: Joyce H. Corrington, John William Corrington, from the book
   Sister of the Road by Boxcar Bertha Thompson as told to Ben
   Reitman
Cinematography: John Stephens
Editing: Buzz Feitshans
Music: Gib Guilbeau, Thad Maxwell
Sound: Don F. Johnson

Producer: Roger Corman
Distributor: American International

Cast: Barbara Hershey (Bertha), David Carradine (Bill Shelley), Barry Primus (Rake Brown), Bernie Casey (Von Morton), John Carradine (H. Buckram Sartoris), David R. Osterhout, Victor Argo (the McIvers), Grahame Pratt (Emeric Pressburger), Chicken Holleman (Michael Powell), Marianne Dolc (Mrs. Mailer), Harry Northup (Harvey Hall), Joe Reynolds (Joe), Martin Scorsese, Gayne Rescher (clients in brothel).

MEAN STREETS (1973)

Direction: Martin Scorsese
Script: Martin Scorsese, Mardik Martin
Cinematography: Kent Wakeford
Editing: Sid Levin
Sound: Glen Glenn
Producer: Jonathan Taplin
Distributor: Warner Bros.

Cast: Harvey Keitel (Charlie), Robert De Niro (Johnny Boy), David Proval (Tony), Amy Robinson (Teresa), Richard Romanus (Michael), Cesare Danova (Giovanni), George Memmoli (Joey Catucci), Victor Argo (Mario), Lenny Scaletta (Jimmy), Murray Moston (Oscar), David Carradine (drunk), Robert Carradine (assassin), Jeannie Bell (Diane), Lois Walden (Jewish girl in bar), D' Mitch Davis (black cop), Dino Seragusa (old man), Julie Andelman (girl Charlie dances with at party), Peter Fain (George), Harry Northup (soldier), Robert Wilder (Benton), Jaime Alba (first young boy), Ken Konstantin (second young boy), Nicki "Ack" Aquiulino (man on docks), Catherine Scorsese (woman on landing), Ken Sinclair (Sammy), B. Mitchell Reed (disc jockey), Martin Scorsese (Michael's hired killer).

ALICE DOESN'T LIVE HERE ANYMORE (1974)

Direction: Martin Scorsese
Script: Robert Getchell

Cinematography: Kent Wakeford
Editing: Marcia Lucas
Music: Richard Lasalle
Sound: Don Parker
Production Design: Toby Carr Rafelson
Producers: David Susskind, Audrey Maas
Distributor: Warner Bros.

Cast: Ellen Burstyn (Alice Hyatt), Kris Kristofferson (David), Alfred
Lutter (Tommy), Diane Lad (Flo), Billy Green Bush (Donald), Vic
Tayback (Mel), Jodie Foster (Audrey), Harvey Keitel (Ben), Lelia
Goldoni (Bea), Lane Bradbury (Rita), Valeria Curtin (Vera), Harry
Northup (bartender), Murray Moston (Jacobs), Mia Bendixsen (Alice
at age 8), Ola Moore (old woman), Dean Casper (Chicken), Henry M.
Kendrick (shop assistant), Martin Brinton (Lenny), Mardik Martin
(customer in club during Alice's audition), Martin Scorsese, Larry
Cohen (patrons in diner).

TAXI DRIVER (1976)

Direction: Martin Scorsese
Script: Paul Schrader
Cinematography: Michael Chapman
Editing: Marcia Lucas, Tom Rolf, Melvin Shapiro
Music: Bernard Herrmann
Art Direction: Charles Rosen
Special Make-up: Dick Smith
Producers: Michael Phillips, Julia Phillips
Distributor: Columbia Pictures

Cast: Robert De Niro (Travis Bickle), Jodie Foster (Iris), Cybill
Shepherd (Betsy), Harvey Keitel (Sport), Steven Prince (Andy, the gun
salesman), Albert Brooks (Tom), Peter Boyle (Wizard), Leonard Harris
(Charles Palantine), Diahnne Abbott (woman at concession stand in
porno theater), Frank Adu (angry black man), Richard Higgs (secret
service agent at Palantine rallies), Gino Ardito (policeman at rally),
Garth Avery (Iris's companion), Copper Cunningham (prostitute in
cab), Harry Fischler (cab dispatcher), Harry Cohn (cabbie in
Bellmore), Brenda Dickson (woman in soap opera), Nat Grant (stick-up

man), Robert Maroff (mafioso), Beau Kayser (man on soap opera), Vic
Magnotta (secret service photographer), Norman Matlock (Charlie T.),
Murray Moston (caretaker at Iris's apartment house), Harry Northup
(soldier), Bill Minkin (Tom's assistant), Gene Palma (street drummer),
Peter Savage (the john), Robert Shields (Palantine aide), Robin Utt
(campaign worker), Joe Spinell (personnel officer), Maria Turner
(angry prostitute on street), Carey Poe (campaign worker), Ralph
Singleton (television interviewer), Martin Scorsese (angry man with gun
in Travis's cab).

NEW YORK, NEW YORK (1977)

Direction: Martin Scorsese
Script: Earl Mac Rauch, Mardik Martin, from a story by Earl Mac
    Rauch
Cinematography: Laszlo Kovacs
Editing: Tom Rolf, B. Lovitt
Original music and songs: John Kander and Fred Ebb
Production Design: Boris Leven
Producers: Irwin Winkler, Robert Chartoff
Distributor: United Artists

Cast: Robert De Niro (Jimmy Doyle), Liza Minnelli (Francine Evans),
Lionel Stander (Tony Harwell), Barry Primus (Paul Wilson), Mary Kay
Place (Bernice), Georgie Auld (Frankie Harte), George Memmoli
(Nicky), Dick Miller (Palm Club owner), Murray Moston (Horace
Morris), Lenie Gaines (Artie Kirks), Clarence Clemons (Cecil Powell),
Kathi McGinnis (Ellen Flannery), Norman Palmer (desk clerk), Adam
David Winkler (Jimmy Doyle, Jr.), Dimitri Logothetis (desk clerk),
Frank Sivera (Eddie di Muzio), Diahnne Abbott (Harlem club singer),
Margo Winkler (argumentative woman), Steven Prince (record
producer), Don Calfa (Gilbert), Bernie Kuby (Justice of the Peace), Bill
Baldwin (announcer in Moonlit Terrace), Mary Lindsay (hatcheck girl
in Meadows), Jon Cutler (musician in Frankie Harte's band), Nicky
Blair (cab driver), Casey Kasem (D.J.), Jay Salerno (bus driver),
William Tole (Tommy Dorsey), Sydney Guilaroff (hairdresser), Peter
Savage (Horace Morris's assistant), Gene Castle (dancing sailor), Louie
Guss (Fowler), Shera Danese (Doyle's girl in Major Chord), Bill
McMillan (D.J.), David Nichols (Arnold Trench), Harry Northup

(Alabama), Mart Zagon (manager of South Bend Ballroom), Timothy Blake (nurse), Betty Cole (chairwoman), De Forest Covan (porter), Phil Gray (trombone player in Doyle's band), Roosevelt Smith (bouncer in Major Chord), Bruce L. Lucoff (cab driver), Bill Phillips Murray (waiter in Harlem club), Clint Arnold (trombone player in Palm Club), Richard Alan Berk (drummer in Palm Club), Wilfred R. Middlebrooks (bass player in Palm Club), Jake Vernon Porter (trumpet player in Palm Club), Nat Pierce (piano player in Palm Club), Manuel Escobosa (fighter in Moonlit Terrace), Susan Kay Hunt, Teryn Jenkins (girls at Moonlit Terrace), Mardik Martin (well-wisher at Moonlit Terrace), Leslie Summers (woman in black at Moonlit Terrace), Brick Michaels (man at table at Moonlit Terrace), Washington Rucker, Booty Reed (musicians at hiring hall), David Armstrong, Robert Buckingham, Eddie Garrett, Nico Stevens (reporters), Peter Fain (greeter in Up Club), Angelo Lamonea (waiter in Up Club), Charles A. Tamburro, Wallace McClesky (bouncers in Up Club), Ronald Prince (dancer in Up Club), Robert Petersen (photographer), Richard Raymond (railroad conductor), Hank Robinson (Francine's bodyguard), Harold Ross (cab driver), Eddie Smith (man in bathroom at Harlem club).

THE LAST WALTZ (1978)

Direction: Martin Scorsese
Cinematography: Michael Chapman, Laszlo Kovacs, Vilmos Zsig-
            mond, David Myers, Bobby Byrne, Michael Watkins, Hiro
            Narita
Editing: Yeu-Bun Lee, Jan Roblee
Music Editors: Ken Wannenberg, Bob Raff
Concert Audio: Rob Fraboni
Concert Producer: Bill Graham
Production Design: Boris Leven
Producer: Robbie Robertson
Distributor: Warner Bros.

Interviewer: Martin Scorsese
Performers: Ronnie Hawkins, Dr. John, Neil Young, The Staples,
            Neil Diamond, Joni Mitchell, Paul Butterfield, Muddy Waters,
            Eric Clapton, Emmylou Harris, Van Morrison, Bob Dylan,
            Ringo Starr, Ron Wood.

The Band: Robbie Robertson, Rick Danko, Levon Helm, Garth Hudson, Richard Manuel.

RAGING BULL (1980)

Direction: Martin Scorsese
Script: Paul Schrader, Mardik Martin, from the book *Raging Bull* by Jake La Motta with Joseph Carter and Peter Savage
Cinematography: Michael Chapman
Editing: Thelma Schoonmaker
Music: From pre-recorded classical and popular sources
Sound: Les Lazarowitz, Michael Evje, Donald W. Mitchell, Bill Nicholson, David J. Kimball
Producers: Irwin Winkler, Robert Chartoff
Distributor: United Artists

Cast: Robert De Niro (Jake La Motta), Cathy Moriarty (Vickie La Motta), Joe Pesci (Joey La Motta), Frank Vincent (Salvy), Nicholas Colasanto (Tommy Como), Theresa Saldana (Lenore), Mario Gallo (Mario), Frank Adonis (Patsy), Joseph Bono (Guido), Frank Topham (Toppy), Lori Anne Flax (Irma), Charles Scorsese (Charlie, man with Como), Don Dunphy (himself), Bill Hanrahan (Eddie Eagan), Rita Bennett (Emma, Miss 48's), James V. Christy (Dr. Pinto), Bernie Allen (comedian), Michael Badalucco (soda fountain clerk), Thomas Beansy Lobasso (Beansy), Paul Forrest (Monsignor), Peter Petrella (Johnny), Sal Serafino Thomassetti (Webster Hall bouncer), Geraldine Smith (Janet), Mardik Martin (Copa waiter), Maryjane Lauria (1st girl), Linda Artuso (2nd girl), Peter Savage (Jackie Curtie), Daniel P. Conte (Detroit promoter), Joe Malanga (bodyguard), Sabine Turco, Jr., Steve Orlando, Silvia Garcia, Jr. (bouncers at Copa), John Arceri (maitre d'), Joseph A. Morale (1st man at table), James Dimodica (2nd man at table), Robert Uricola (man outside cab), Andrea Orlando (woman in cab), Allan Malamud (reporter at Jake's house), D.J. Blair (State Attorney Bronson), Laura James (Mrs. Bronson), Richard McMurray (J.R.), Mary Albee (underage ID girl), Liza Katz (woman with ID girl), Candy Moore (Linda), Richard A. Berk (1st musician), Theodore Saunders (2nd musician), Noah Young (3rd musician), Nick Trisko (bartender Carlo), Lou Tiano (Ricky), Rob Evan Collins (1st arresting deputy), Wally Berns (2nd arresting deputy), Allan Joseph (jeweller), Bob Aaron (1st prison guard), Glen Leigh Marshall (2nd prison guard), Martin Scorsese (Barbizon stagehand), Reeves Fight: Floyd Anderson (Jimmy Reeves), Gene Lebell (ring announcer), Harold Valan (referee), Victor Magnotta (fighting soldier); 1st Robinson Fight: Johnny Barnes ("Sugar" Ray Robinson), John Thomas (trainer), Kenny Davis (referee), Paul Carmello (ring announcer); 2nd Robinson Fight: Jimmy Lennon (ring announcer), Bobby Rings (referee); Janiro Fight: Kevin Mahon (Tony Janiro), Martin Denkin (referee), Shay Duffin (ring announcer); Fox Fight: Eddie Mustaffa Muhammad (Billy Fox), "Sweet" Dick Whittington (ring announcer), Jack Lotz (referee), Kevin Breslin (heckler); Cerdan Fight: Louis Raftis (Marcel Cerdan), Frank Shain (ring announcer), Coley Wallace (Joe Louis), Fritzie Higgins (woman with Vickie), George Latka (referee), Fred Dennis (1st cornerman), Robert B. Loring (2nd cornerman); Dauthille Fight: Johnny Turner (Laurent Turner), Jimmy Lennon (ring announcer), Vern de Paul (Dauthille's trainer), Chuck Hassett (referee), Ken Richards (reporter at phonebooth), Peter Fain (Dauthille cornerman); 3rd Robinson Fight: Count Billy Varga (ring announcer), Harvy Parry (referee), Ted Husing (TV announcer).

THE KING OF COMEDY (1983)

Direction: Martin Scorsese
Script: Paul D. Zimmerman
Cinematography: Fred Schuler
Editing: Thelma Schoonmaker
Music Production: Robbie Robertson
Supervising Sound Editor: Frank Warner
Producer: Arnon Milchan
Distributor: Twentieth Century-Fox

Cast: Robert De Niro (Rupert Pupkin), Jerry Lewis (Jerry Langford), Diahnne Abbott (Rita), Sandra Bernhard (Masha), Ed Herlihy (himself), Lou Brown (bandleader), Loretta Tupper, Peter Potulski, Vinnie Gonzales (stage door fans), Whitey Ryan (stage door guard), Doc Lawless (chauffeur), Marta Heflin (young girl), Catherine Scorsese (Rupert's mom), Cathy Scorsese (Dolores), Chuck Low (man in Chinese restaurant), Margo Winkler (receptionist), Shelley Hack (Cathy Long), Mick Jones, Joe Strummer, Paul Simonon, Kosmo Vynil, Ellen

Foley, Pearl Harbour, Gabu Salter, Jerry Baxter-Worman, Dom Letis (street scum), Fred De Cordova (Bert Thomas), Edgar J. Scherick (Wilson Crockett), Kim Chan (Jonno), Dr. Joyce Brothers, Victor Borge, Tony Randall (themselves), Jay Julien (Langford's lawyer), Harry Ufland (Langford's agent), Martin Scorsese (television director).

AFTER HOURS (1985)

Direction: Martin Scorsese
Script: Joseph Minion
Cinematography: Michael Ballhaus
Editing: Thelma Schoonmaker
Music: Howard Shore
Production Design: Jeffrey Townsend
Producers: Amy Robinson, Griffin Dunne, Robert E. Colesberry
Distributor: Warner Bros.

Cast: Rosanna Arquette (Marcy), Verna Bloom (June), Thomas Chong (Pepe), Griffin Dunne (Paul Hackett), Linda Fiorentino (Kiki), Teri Garr (Julie), John Heard (Tom the bartender), Cheech Marin (Neil), Catherine O'Hara (Gail), Dick Miller (waiter), Will Patton (Horst), Robert Plunkett (street pickup), Clark Evans, Victor Bumbalo, Bill Elverman (neighbors), Joel Jason, Rand Carr (bikers), Clarence Feeder (bouncer), Harry Baker (Jett), Margo Winkler (woman with gun), Victor Magnotta (dead man), Robin Johnson (punk girl), Stephen J. Lim (chief Berlin Bartender), Frank Aquilino, Marce Catalino, Paula Raflo, Rockets Redglare (angry mob members).

MIRROR, MIRROR (1985)

Direction: Martin Scorsese
Script: Joseph Minion, Steven Spielberg
Cinematography: Robert Stevens
Editing: Jo Ann Fogle
Music: Michael Kamen
Production Design: Rick Cantor
Producer: David E. Vogel
Distributor: Universal Pictures

Cast: Sam Waterston (Jordan), Helen Shaver (Karen), Dick Cavett (himself), Tim Robbins (phantom), Dana Gladstone (producer), Valerie Greer (host), Michael C. Gwynne (jail attendant), Peter Iacangelo (limo driver), Jonathan Luna (cameraman), Harry Northup (security guard), Glenn Scarpelli (Jeffrey Gelb), Jack Thibeua (tough guy).

THE COLOR OF MONEY (1986)

Direction: Martin Scorsese
Script: Richard Price
Cinematography: Michael Ballhaus
Editing: Thelma Schoonmaker
Music: Robbie Robertson
Production Design: Boris Leven
Producers: Irving Axelrod, Barbara De Fina
Distributor: Touchstone Pictures

Cast: Paul Newman (Eddie), Tom Cruise (Vincent), Mary Elizabeth Mastrantonio (Carmen), Helen Shaver (Janelle), John Turturro (Julian), Bill Cobbs (Orvis), Robert Agins (Earl at Chalkies), Alvin Anastasia (Kennedy), Randall Arney (Child World customer #1), Elizabeth Bracco (Diane at bar), Vito D' Ambrosio (Lou in Child World), Ron Dean (guy in crowd), Lisa Dodson (Child World customer #2), Donald A. Feeney (referee), Paul Geier ("Two Brothers/Stranger" player), Carey Goldenberg (congratulating spectator), Joe Guastaferro (Chuck the bartender), Paul Herman (player in casino bar), Mark Jarvis (guy at Janelle's), Lawrence Linn (congratulating spectator), Keith McCready (Grady Seasons), Jimmy Mataya (Julian's friend in green room), Grady Mathews (Dud), Carol Messing (casino bar band singer/Julian's girl), Steve Mizerak (Duke, Eddie's first opponent), Rick Mohr (congratulating spectator), Lloyd Moss (narrator—Resorts International), Michael Nash (Moselle's opponent), Mario Nieves (third Latin guy), Miguel A. Nino (first Latin guy), Andy Nolfo (referee #2), Ernest Perry, Jr. (eye doctor), Jerry Piller (Tom), Iggy Pop (skinny player on the road), Richard Price (guy who calls Dud), Juan Ramirez (second Latin guy), Alex Ross (bartender who bets), Peter Saxe (casino bar band member), Charles Scorsese (high roller #1), Rodrick Selby (congratulating spectator), Christina Siegel (waitress), Harold L. Simonsen (chief justice at tournament), Fred Squillo (high roller #2),

Brian Sunina (casino bar band member), Wanda Christine (casino clerk), Forest Witaker (Amos), Jim Widlowski (casino bar band member), Bruce A. Young (Moselle), Zoe (dog Walkby).

THE LAST TEMPTATION OF CHRIST (1988)

Direction: Martin Scorsese
Script: Paul Schrader, based on the novel by Nikos Kazantzakis
Cinematography: Michael Ballhaus
Editing: Thelma Schoonmaker
Music: Peter Gabriel
Production Design: John Beard
Costumes: Jean Pierre Delifer
Makeup Supervision: Manlio Rocchetti
Producer: Barbara De Fina
Distributor: Universal Pictures

Cast: Willem Dafoe (Jesus), Harvey Keitel (Judas), Paul Greco (zealot), Steven Shill (centurion), Verna Bloom (Mary, mother of Jesus), Barbara Hershey (Mary Magdalene), Roberts Blossom (aged master), Barry Miller (Jeroboam), Gary Basaraba (James apostle), Irvin Kershner (Zebedae), Victor Argo (Peter apostle), Michael Been (John apostle), Leo Burmesiter (Nathanael apostle), Andre Gregory (John the Baptist), Peggy Gormley (Martha, sister of Lazarus), Randy Danson (Mary, sister of Lazarus), Robert Stafford (man at wedding), Doris van Thury (woman with Mary, mother of Jesus), Thomas Arana (Lazarus), Alan Rosenberg (Thomas apostle), Del Russell (money changer), Nehemiah Persoff (rabbi), Donald Hudson (sadducee), Peter Berling (beggar), Harry Dean Stanton (Saint Paul), David Bowie (Pontius Pilate), Juliette Caton (girl angel), Penny Brown, Gabriel Ford, Dale Wyatt, Domenico Fiore, Tomas Arana, Ted Rusoff, Leo Damian, Robert Laconi, Jonathan Zhivago, Ileana Douglas (voices in crowd). Khalbib Benchoub, Redouane Fahane, Fabienne Fanciatili, Naima Skikes, Squad Rahal, Othrane Chbani Idrissi, Jamal Belkhayat (dancers).

LIFE LESSONS (1989)

Direction: Martin Scorsese
Script: Richard Price
Cinematography: Freddie Francis
Executive Producers: Jack Rollins, Charles H. Joffe
Producer: Robert Greenhut
Distributor: Buena Vista

Cast: Nick Nolte (Lionel Dobie), Patrick O'Neal (Philip Fowler), Rosanna Arquette (Paulette), Phil Harper (businessman), Kenneth J. McGregor, David Cryer, Paul Geier (suits), Jesse Borrego (Reuben Toro), Gregorij von Leitis (Kurt Bloom), Steve Buscemi (Gregory Stark), Lenardo (woman at Blind Alley), Peter Gabriel (himself), Mark Boone, Jr. (Hank), Ileana Douglas (Paulette's friend), Deborah Harry (girl at Blind Alley), Paul Herman, Victor Argo (cops), Victor Trull (maitre d'), Richard Price (artist at opening).

GOODFELLAS (1990)

Director: Martin Scorsese
Script: Nicholas Pileggi, Martin Scorsese, based on the novel
       Wiseguys by Nicholas Pileggi
Cinematography: Michael Ballhaus
Editing: Thelma Schoonmaker
Music Editor: Christopher Brooks
Production Design: Kristi Zea
Producer: Irwin Winkler
Distributor: Warner Bros.

Cast: Robert De Niro (Jimmy Conway), Ray Liotta (Henry Hill), Joe Pesci (Tommy De Vito), Lorraine Bracco (Karen Hill), Paul Sorvino (Paul Cicero), Frank Sivero (Frankie Carbone), Tony Darrow (Sonny Bunz), Mike Starr (Frenchy), Frank Vincent (Billy Batts), Chick Low (Morris Kessler), Frank Dileo (Tuddy Cicero), Henny Youngman (himself), Gina Mastrogiacomo (Janice Rossi), Catherine Scorsese (Tommy's mother), Charles Scorsese (Vinnie), Suzanne Shepherd (Karen's mother), Debi Mozar (Sandy), Margo Winkler (Belle Kessler), Walker White (Lois Byrd), Jerry Vale (himself), Julie Carfeld

(Mickey Conway), Christopher Serrone (young Henry), Elaine Kagan (Henry's mother), Beau Starr (Henry's father), Kevin Corrigan (Michael Hill), Michael Imperioli (Spider), Robbie Vinton (Bobbie Vinton), John Williams (Johnny Roastbeef), Daniel P. Conte (Dr. Dan), Tony Conforti (Tony), Frank Pellegrino (Johnny Dio), Ronald Maccone (Ronnie), Tony Sirico (Tony Stacks), Joseph D'Onofrio (young Tommy), Steve Forleo (city detective 1), Richard Dioguard (city detective 2), Frank Adonis (Anthony Stabile), John Manca (Micky Eyes), Joseph Bono (Mikey Franzese), Katherine Wallach (Diane), Mark Evan Jacobs (Bruce), Angela Pietropinto (Cicero's wife), Marianne Leone (Tuddy's wife), Marie Michaels (Mrs. Carbone), Lo Nardo (Frenchy's wife), Samuel L. Jackson (Stacks Edwards).

CAPE FEAR (1991)

Direction: Martin Scorsese
Script: Wesley Strick
Cinematography: Freddie Francis
Editing: Thelma Schoonmaker
Music: Bernard Herrmann, orchestrated by Elmer Bernstein
Production Design: Henry Bumstead
Producer: Barbara De Fina
Distributor: Universal Pictures

Cast: Robert De Niro (Max Cady), Nick Nolte (Sam Bowden), Jessica Lange (Leigh Bowden), Juliette Lewis (Danielle Bowden), Joe Don Baker (Claude Kersek), Robert Mitchum (Lt. Elgart), Gregory Peck (Lee Heller), Martin Balsam (judge), Ileana Douglas (Lori Davis), Fred Dalton Thompson (Tom Broadbent), Zully Montero (Graciela), Craig Henne, Forest Burton, E.A. Poe IV, W. Paul Bade (prisoners), Joel Kolker, Antoni Corone (corrections officers), Tamara Jones (ice cream cashier), Roger Prehto, Ferris Buckner (racquetball colleagues), Margit Moreland (secretary), Will Knickerbocker (detective), Robert L. Gerlach, Bruce E. Heldstein (arresting officers), Richard Wasserman, Paul Nagle, Jr., Paul Froemler, Mary Ellen O'Brien, Jody Wilson (parade watchers), Kate Colburn (waitress), Domenica Scorsese (Danny's girlfriend), Gar Stephen (big man), Billy Lucas (big man #2), Ken Collins (big man #3), Linda Perri, Elizabeth Moyer (ticket agents),

Catherine and Charles Scorsese (fruit stand customers), Jackie Davis (Jimmy the dockmaster).

THE AGE OF INNOCENCE (1992)

Direction: Martin Scorsese
Script: Jay Cocks, Martin Scorsese, based on the novel by Edith Wharton
Cinematography: Michael Ballhaus
Editing: Thelma Schoonmaker
Music: Elmer Bernstein
Production Design: Dante Ferreti
Costume Design: Gabriella Pesucci
Producer: Barbara De Fina
Distributor: Columbia Pictures

Cast: Daniel Day-Lewis (Newland Archer), Michelle Pfeiffer (Ellen Olenska), Winona Ryder (May Welland), Linda Faye Farkas (female opera singer), Michael Rees Davis, Terry Cook, Jon Garrison (male opera singers), Richard E. Grant (Larry Lefferts), Alec McCowen (Sillerton Jackson), Geraldine Chaplin (Mrs. Welland), Mary Beth Hurt (Regina Beaufort), Stuart Wilson (Julius Beaufort), Howard Erskine (Beaufort guest), John McLoughlin, Christopher Nilsson (party guests), Miriam Margoyles (Mrs. Mingott), Sian Phillips (Mrs. Archer), Carolyn Farina (Janey Archer), Michael Gough (Henry van der Luyden), Alexis Smith (Louisa van der Luyden), Kevin Sanders (the Duke), W. B. Brydon (Mrs. Urban Dagonet), Tracey Ellis (Gertrude Lefferts), Cristina Pronzati (Countess Olsenska's maid), Clement Fowler (florist), Norman Lloyd (Mr. Letterblair), Cindy Katz (stage actress), Thomas Gibson (stage actor), Zoe (herself), Jonathan Pryce (Riviere), June Squibb (Mingott maid), Domenica Scorsese (Katie Blendker), Mac Orange (Archer maid), Brian Davies (Philip), Thomas Barbour (Archer guest), Henry Fehren (Bishop), Patricia Dunnock (Mary Archer), Robert Sean Leonard (Ted Archer), Joanne Woodward (narrator).

SHORT FILMS

WHAT'S A NICE GIRL LIKE YOU DOING IN A PLACE LIKE
THIS? (1963)

Direction: Martin Scorsese
Script: Martin Scorsese
Cinematography: James Newman
Editing: Robert Hunsicker
Music: Richard H. Cole; lyrics by Sandor Reich
Sound: Sandor Reich
Produced by the New York University Department of Television,
     Motion Pictures, and Radio

Cast: Zeph Michaelis (Harry), Mimi Stark (wife), Sarah Braverman
(analyst), Fred Sica (friend), Robert Uricola (singer).

IT'S NOT JUST YOU, MURRAY (1964)

Direction: Martin Scorsese
Script: Martin Scorsese, Mardik Martin
Cinematography: Richard Coll
Editing: Eli Bleich
Art Direction: Lancelot Braithwaite, Victor Magnotta
Produced by the New York University Department of Television,
     Motion Pictures, and Radio

Cast: Ira Rubin (Murray), Andrea Martin (the wife), Sam De Fazio
(Joe), Robert Uricola (the singer), Catherine Scorsese (the mother),
Victor Magnotta, Richard Sweeton, Mardik Martin, John Bivona,
Bernard Weisberger.

THE BIG SHAVE (1967-1968)

Direction: Martin Scorsese
Script: Martin Scorsese

Cinematography: Arres Demertzis
Music: Bunny Berrigan
Sponsored by the Cinematheque Royale de Belgique

Cast: Peter Bernuth (young man).

ITALIAN AMERICAN (1974)

Direction: Martin Scorsese
Treatment: Mardik Martin, Larry Cohen
Cinematography: Alex Hirschfeld
Editing: B. Lovitt
Sound: Lee Osborne
Producers: Saul Rubin, Elaine Attias

Cast: Catherine, Charles, and Martin Scorsese.

AMERICAN BOY: A PROFILE OF STEVEN PRINCE (1978)

Direction: Martin Scorsese
Treatment: Mardik Martin, Julia Cameron
Cinematography: Michael Chapman
Editing: Amy Jones, Bertram Lovitt
Sound: Darin Knight
Producer: Bertram Lovitt

Cast: Steven Prince, Martin Scorsese, Mardik Martin, George
Memmoli, Julia Cameron, Kathy McGinnis.

INDEX

ABOUT THE AUTHOR

A Ph.D. in English from the University of Minnesota, Michael Bliss teaches English and film at Virginia Polytechnic Institute and State University. His books include *Brian De Palma*; *Martin Scorsese and Michael Cimino*; *Justified Lives: Morality and Narrative in the Films of Sam Peckinpah*; *Doing It Right: The Best Criticism on Sam Peckinpah's "The Wild Bunch"*; and the forthcoming co-authored study *What Goes Around Comes Around: The Films of Jonathan Demme*. At present, Bliss is completing three books, *Dreams Within a Dream: Australian Cinema and the Films of Peter Weir* and two co-authored works: *Hong Kong Cinema: Past and Present* and an illustrated volume on the making of "The Wild Bunch."